T0330662

Disrupting Mainstream Journalism in India

Disrupting Mainstream Journalism in India offers a comprehensive and empirically-grounded analysis of the production of digital journalism by marginalized groups within Indian society.

Drawing on in-depth interviews with practitioners as well as samples of news content, the author critically examines the way in which varied forms of digital alternative journalism provide socially, economically and politically disadvantaged groups with new and unprecedented opportunities to express their own perspectives, as well as offering alternatives to the hegemony of mainstream news narratives. These marginalized groups include women, Dalits and Muslims whose voices tend to be erased or misrepresented within the public sphere. By exploring these disruptions, Chadha offers insight into not only the new media landscape of India but also its implications for journalism and democracy at large.

Disrupting Mainstream Journalism in India is a valuable empirical resource for students and scholars interested in Indian media, journalism and democracy.

Kalyani Chadha is an associate professor at Northwestern University's Medill School of Journalism, Media, Integrated Marketing Communications. Her research focuses on the media and journalism landscape in India, with a recent emphasis on the rise of various forms of digital journalism, both right wing and outlets aimed at marginalized groups. Her work has appeared in numerous prestigious journals, including *Digital Journalism and Journalism Studies* as well as several edited collections. She recently co-edited a collection titled *Newswork and Precarity* published by Routledge. She serves on the editorial boards of Digital Journalism, Journalism Practice and Mass Communication and Society.

Disruptions: Studies in Digital Journalism
Series editor: Bob Franklin

Disruptions refers to the radical changes provoked by the affordances of digitaltechnologies that occur at a pace and on a scale that disrupts settled understandings and traditional ways of creating value, interacting and communicating both socially and professionally. The consequences for digital journalism involve far reaching changes to business models, professional practices, roles, ethics, products and even challenges to the accepted definitions and understandings of journalism. For Digital Journalism Studies, the field of academic inquiry which explores and examines digital journalism, disruption results in paradigmatic and tectonic shifts in scholarly concerns. It prompts reconsideration of research methods, theoretical analyses and responses (oppositional and consensual) to such changes, which have been described as being akin to 'a moment of mind-blowing uncertainty'.

Routledge's book series, *Disruptions: Studies in Digital Journalism*, seeks to capture, examine and analyse these moments of exciting and explosive professional and scholarly innovation which characterize developments in the day-to-day practice of journalism in an age of digital media, and which are articulated in the newly emerging academic discipline of Digital Journalism Studies.

For more information about this series, please visit: www.routledge.com/Disruptions/book-series/DISRUPTDIGJOUR

Disrupting Mainstream Journalism in India

The Rise of Alternative
Journalisms Online

Kalyani Chadha

Routledge
Taylor & Francis Group

LONDON AND NEW YORK

First published 2025
by Routledge
4 Park Square, Milton Park, Abingdon, Oxon OX14 4RN

and by Routledge
605 Third Avenue, New York, NY 10158

Routledge is an imprint of the Taylor & Francis Group, an informa business

British Library Cataloguing-in-Publication Data
A catalogue record for this book is available from the British Library

ISBN: 978-1-032-15447-3 (hbk)
ISBN: 978-1-032-15454-1 (pbk)
ISBN: 978-1-003-24420-2 (ebk)

DOI: 10.4324/9781003244202

Typeset in Times New Roman
by KnowledgeWorks Global Ltd.

To my family

Aamir, Promila, Samir and Vimal.

Contents

Figures

Acknowledgments

Special thanks to the many journalists who agreed to be interviewed and gave so generously of their time and expertise. The author would also like to thank the Association for Education in Journalism and Mass Communication (AEJMC) for awarding her the Senior Scholar Grant to support her work.

1 India's Contemporary News Media Landscape

Structural Challenges, Their Implications and Responses

Introduction

Over the past three decades, India's news media landscape has experienced transformative changes reflected most visibly in the proliferation of news outlets across different media forms. Currently, the country has almost 15,000 registered newspapers, 392 television news channels—mainly in the form of privately-owned regional language stations—(Krishnan, 2021) as well as over 800 million internet users (Basuroy, 2022). This expansion of the country's media system began in the 1990s, when facing an internal financial crisis, India embarked on a course of neo-liberal, market-oriented policy reforms. This shift, which resulted in the emergence of new goods and services as well as middle class consumers who could be targeted by advertisers, combined with limited governmental regulation of newly available communication technologies such as cable and satellite services, provided a powerful stimulus to the country's media industry. While the bulk of the initial expansion occurred in the print and broadcast arenas, during the past decade, aided by cheap smartphones and declining data costs, exponential growth has also come to characterize the digital media sector, with Indians emerging as major consumers of online content, including news (Basuroy, 2022). By one recent estimate, online consumption of news (including on social media) in India stands at 72% of the population, with television and print following at 49% and 40%, respectively (Krishnan, 2023).

Concomitantly, the growth of the Indian news media sector has also engendered a celebratory narrative around the industry (Chadha, 2017). Indeed, it is often asserted that in contrast to the Global North where the migration of advertising revenues and audiences to social media platforms has produced a contraction of mainstream journalism, legacy news organizations continue to have a dominant presence in the Indian news landscape (Khanna, 2022).[1] According to the Reuters Institute Digital News Report, so-called "legacy brands in broadcast and print…were the top news sources attracting viewers online and offline" (Krishnan, 2023). But even as the Indian news industry has experienced what Hallin and Mancini (1994) term "the triumph of the liberal model,"

DOI: 10.4324/9781003244202-1

(p. 251)—it is characterized by wide-ranging economic and political challenges that affect the practice of journalism (Chadha, 2017; Chadha & Arya, 2021).

Economic and Political Challenges

Notable among such challenges is the overwhelming pressure from market imperatives. As the Press Council of India, an autonomous body overseeing the news media sector, has stated, the primary aim of most Indian media companies "is to maximize profits and returns to shareholders" (2010, p. 10). However, despite a rapid growth trajectory or perhaps because of it, the financial foundations of India's news media industry remain unstable (Krishnan, 2021) "with only a few market leaders operating profitably and large numbers of second- and third-tier companies in each market lucky merely to survive" (Jain, 2015, p. 163). With profitability a defining concern, many news organizations have sought to bolster their bottom line through commercial "innovations" such as the growing placement of advertorials or "sponsored content" as well as the creation of "private treaties" or strategic partnerships whereby news outlets offer corporations discounted advertising in return for "equity deals, real estate exchanges or royalty linked payments" (Sharma, 2013, p. 2).

Along with such pervasive hyper-commercialism, the Indian media market is simultaneously characterized both by rising levels of national and regional media concentration and by the presence of powerful media conglomerates (Reporters without Borders, 2018). For example, the top four dailies in the English and Hindi language markets control more than 75% audience in these respective languages (Reporters without Borders, 2018). Also commonplace in the Indian context is the investment by non-media corporations in the news sector as well as the acquisition of non-media businesses by media corporations. Though this trend is by no means new, it has become increasingly manifest in recent years, with the country's leading industrial conglomerates such as Reliance and Adani Enterprises purchasing stakes in media companies (Vengattil, 2022). Meanwhile, media entities such as DB Corporation that owns India's most widely circulated Hindi paper, *Dainik Bhaskar*, have acquired interests in mining, manufacturing and real estate (Chadha, 2017). These developments in the Indian context have been facilitated by factors such as relationships with political elites well as the virtual absence of regulatory controls. As Thomas (2010) explains:

> Media expansion in India has occurred within a policy environment that ironically is bereft of substantial policy... this environment has been of particular benefit to the larger media houses who have used their economic and political muscle to strengthen their dominance in cross sectoral media markets. (p. 14)

Additionally, the Indian news landscape is also defined by the rampant politicization of media ownership, with politicians, their families or their proxies acquiring stakes in a variety of news media outlets. In this context, the Media Ownership Monitor project—which analyzes media ownership patterns in countries that score low on the World Press Freedom Index—found that among 58 leading media outlets in India, ten had "direct or indirect links with politics," and that there were "countless others...who refused to declare their political affiliations, but yet own media companies" (Sam, 2019). In fact, by one estimate, almost 80% of India's television news channels are owned by political figures, real estate and investment companies (Outlook Web Desk, 2022).

At the same time, the Indian state—through the exercise of both legal and financial power—continues to play a powerful role in controlling the news media sector. For instance, numerous pre-independence laws such as various sections of the Indian Penal Code, including laws against "criminal defamation," "disturbing the public order" and "inciting religious enmity," have been mobilized against journalists at both regional and national levels (Chadha & Arya, 2021). News outlets perceived to be opposed to the government have moreover been targeted under a variety of business-related laws (Joseph, 2002; Sodhi, 2023).

While this practice was certainly prevalent under previous governments, it has grown considerably under the ruling *Bharatiya Janata Party* or BJP as it is popularly known.[2] The administration's control over news outlets has also been strengthened by the latter's dependence on advertising revenues from governmental agencies. Such revenues totaled approximately $800 million between 2014 and 2019 (Maheshwari & Sparks, 2018), with some outlets deriving as much as half of their revenues from state-sponsored advertising (Mohan, 2021). This reliance has become even more pronounced due to the recent economic slowdown caused by the government's economic policies such as demonetization and the introduction of new taxes (Kant, 2019) as well as the COVID-19 pandemic, both of which resulted in demonstrable declines in corporate advertising. Thus, despite claims regarding the size and dynamism of the news industry, the journalistic field in India would appear to be characterized by "heteronomy," rather than "autonomy," with journalism generally being "subservient" to economic and political elites (Maheshwari & Sparks, 2018, p. 2).

Diversity-Related Challenges

In addition to such structural forces, journalistic production is also impacted by the lack of diversity within Indian newsrooms that tend to be dominated by upper caste, male journalists. Indeed, a recent analysis conducted by Oxfam India and media watchdog group *Newslaundry* found that leadership across print, TV and digital media newsrooms was almost exclusively made of upper caste reporters and editors. Similarly, an analysis of bylines showed that most reporters belonged to the upper castes and that not a single Hindi or English newspaper had a Dalit or tribal reporter covering issues pertaining to those marginalized communities. Such exclusionary patterns are also mani-fest across other media as well. For instance, in the case of electronic me-dia, almost 70% of anchors of leading Hindi news shows belong to upper/dominant castes (*Oxfam India-Newslaundry*, 2022). In other words, lower caste or Dalit journalists remain largely absent not only from decision mak-ing positions but also from newsrooms altogether (*Oxfam India-Newslaun-dry*, 2022). Women are also consigned to fairly marginal positions in Indian newsrooms. Another report studying gender representation found that 75% of leadership roles across various types of media organizations were held by men. The situation is especially dismal in the case of Hindi newspapers—read by a significant segment of the Indian population—where less than 10% of women were positioned in senior editorial roles. The report also found significant under-representation of women in broadcast and magazine sec-tors, with only exclusively digital outlets offering somewhat greater gender parity (*Newslaundry*, 2022).

Implications of Structural Challenges for Indian Journalism

Unsurprisingly, these developments have impacted Indian journalism quite negatively. For instance, the supremacy of a market logic has resulted in the privileging of advertiser-friendly news content. This has engendered a "the-matic re-orientation," whereby news organizations have turned away from critical investigations of politics or business and instead shifted toward news related to sports, celebrity and entertainment aimed at younger, urban audi-ences (Rao, 2010). As a result, rural issues—relevant to two-thirds of the Indian population—receive little attention or coverage as do gender issues. According to the UN sponsored report, *Gender Inequality in Indian Media*, just 2.6% of all articles in the country's six leading English dailies and 3% in top Hindi newspapers focused on gender issues (Sharma, 2019). Similarly, Mudgal (2011) who analyzed news content in six leading English and Hindi language dailies, found that only 2% of the coverage of these outlets focused on rural issues. Thus although India ostensibly witnessed a "newspaper revo-lution," in the 1990s when the "marriage of capitalism and technology, carried the experience of print to millions of new readers in small-town and rural India" rural news still "remains on the margins, in the peripheries, it does not reach the center, the larger nation" (Jeffrey, 2000, p. 1), producing what veteran journalist P. Sainath has termed "a disconnect" between the "mass media" and "mass reality" (Naqvi, 2007, p. 18).

Parallel trends are also manifest in the public television broadcaster *Doordarshan*, where declining state support has given rise to a growing reli-ance on the market. Meanwhile, the reporting undertaken by the plethora of regional language newspapers and private television news channels that dot the media landscape, tends to revolve around crime, cricket (India's dominant sport) and cinema (Bollywood) according to Thussu (2007): topics that mainly interest middle class, urban audiences. Such news channels are also characterized by extensive and frequently laudatory coverage of market-oriented policies (Bidwai, 2011) while rarely investigating corporate malfeasance.

This bottom-line orientation reflecting trends long manifest in the West (see for e.g., Franklin, 1997) has also given rise to the growth of infotainment as well as growing tabloidization. Indeed, the "redefinition" of news as a string of startling events is evident in the constant flow of "breaking news alerts" and "sting" operations that are routine features of Indian news broadcasts (Chadha, 2019). Furthermore, in many instances, not only is "sponsored content" often presented using the same format as actual stories, but news organizations are also willing to publish such content as "real stories" for a price (Mazumdar, 2016). This is especially troubling given that audiences are often unable to distinguish sponsored stories from actual news content (Mahajan, 2004).

In addition to hyper-commercialism, trends such as media concentration and cross-media ownership also raise concerns in the Indian context since many states are dominated by single media houses, which exercise considerable control over the production, distribution and content of news. Likewise, the presence of business and political figures in the media sector also poses challenges to independent journalism since such investors generally tend to employ the media outlets they own to advance their own agendas and routinely require their employees to report news in a manner aligned with owners' political orientations or economic interests (Chadha & Koliska, 2016; Jain, 2015). Moreover, through its ability to withhold advertising, the government has also been able to exercise considerable control over news organizations.[3] Confronted by declining advertising revenues and reluctant to lose an important revenue stream, many news organizations have "compromised" by taking down "unfavorable" articles from their sites in order to avoid government anger (Pulla, 2020). Commenting on this trend, media critic Sevanti Ninan has observed that, "since May 2014 when this first government came to power, the 404-error page on media websites is showing up rather more frequently than before" (Ninan, 2019).

In other cases, media owners have intervened to kill stories that are likely to upset the government and even fire journalists who are unwilling to comply with their directives (Chadha & Arya, 2021). As one prominent journalist expressed it, "media proprietors are notorious for reading the tea leaves, they get a clear sense of the tolerance level of politicians in power" (Gopalakrishnan, 2018). In 2018, for example, Prasun Bajpai, a well-known television journalist at ABP, a leading Hindi news channel, stated that the owner of the channel had asked him to refrain from using the prime minister's name or image in conjunction with any criticism of government policies or programs. The journalist also revealed that news content was monitored by the government through a 200-person team that reported to the Ministry of Information and Broadcasting. This team, he said, not only forwarded cases of so-called "problematic" coverage to the appropriate authorities but also sent instructions on how the prime minister was to be covered (Bajpai, 2018).

Mainstream professional journalism in India is thus characterized by numerous structural economic and political forces that inhibit its ability to undertake the tasks normatively associated with the press in a democratic society, namely informing the public, giving voice to underprivileged groups or holding powerful groups and individuals to account. As one veteran journalist and media observer commented, "the media, as it exists and is evolving today, is simply not designed or meant to report on the existing reality of Indian society or inform the public on the economic and political processes at work in it" (Bidwai, 2011).

Responding to Mainstream Media Limitations: The Rise of Alternative Journalisms Online

But while India's mainstream news landscape thus constitutes a troubled terrain, the country's journalistic field is simultaneously witnessing the widespread emergence of alternative forms of journalism in online spaces. Here, the term "alternative journalism" refers to the conventional use of the term as denoting a progressive form of journalism that represents the interests of marginalized groups in society (Atton, 2010).[4] At a technical level, the emergence of such alternative news outlets, which are visible in the form of websites, YouTube channels and social media platform-based entities, has been facilitated by developments such as the cellular revolution and access to mobile internet services that have gained momentum in India since 2010.[5]

In 2001, India had just four million cell phone subscribers, but in the course of a single decade, "the mobile phone was transformed from a rare and unwieldy instrument to a palm-sized, affordable staple, taken for granted by poor fishermen in Kerala and affluent entrepreneurs in Mumbai alike" (Doron & Jeffrey, 2013). In terms of numbers, the country's mobile phone users have grown rapidly and exponentially, rising to 100 million in 2010, 400 million in 2015, reaching almost 750 million users in 2020, with over 744 million accessing the internet via their phones. The latest estimates suggest that India will have one billion smart phone users by 2026 aided by the emergence of the *Jio* network that provides mobile broadband internet access across the nation (Basuroy, 2022).

Launched in 2016 by Indian tycoon Mukesh Ambani, the *Jio* service (which offers extremely low-cost data to consumers) has not only brought millions of new users online but has also transformed consumers' use of cell phones to access online content and services, including news and journalism. According to a recent Reuters Institute report, India has emerged as a mobile-first news market with a significant percentage of those surveyed saying that they only use smartphones for accessing online news and information (Krishnan, 2021).

But even as access to technology has undoubtedly impacted the growth of alternative journalisms in India, a powerful impetus for the emergence of such journalisms has arguably been provided by the failure of legacy media to adequately serve varied marginalized communities in the Indian context. Faced with a general lack of coverage as well as frequent misrepresentation, various subaltern groups in the country have responded by leveraging the affordances of digital technologies to establish their own alternative news outlets. Ranging from identity-focused, advocacy-oriented entities to various types of rurally-based grassroots journalism initiatives, these outlets seek to produce "alternative" journalisms that not only differ from the news produced by professional media organizations—in terms of content and mode of production or sometimes both—but also implicitly challenge the hegemony of mainstream journalism in the context of India.

Alternative Media and Journalism

In the most basic sense, alternative media have been defined as reflecting "views that differ from those of the conventional press" (Streitmatter, 2001, p. xi) or as "any form of media which constitutes an alternative to, or positions itself in opposition to, widely available and consumed mass media products" (Waltz, 2005, p. 2). A few scholars have argued however that such anodyne descriptions undermine any meaningful analysis of the phenomenon (Comedia, 1984), while still others have suggested that the very notion of "alternative media" is "oxymoronic" since "everything is at some point, alternative to something else" (Downing, 2001, p. ix). In response to claims regarding the definitional "vagueness" of the term alternative media, some of those studying such media have sought to provide the notion with greater specificity, typically by conceptualizing alternative media as counter-hegemonic (Payne, 2014). In this regard, Traber (1985), for example, defines alternative media as aiming to bring about "change towards a more equitable social, cultural and economic whole in which the individual is not reduced to an object (of the media or the political powers) but is able to find fulfilment as a total human being" (p. 3). In somewhat similar vein, Downing (2001) defines alternative media in terms of expressing "an alternative vision to hegemonic policies, priorities, and perspectives," while Fuchs (2011) claims that alternative media constitute "mass media that challenge the dominant capitalist forms of media" (p. 298).

Such attempts notwithstanding, alternative media have remained a contested notion with many scholars challenging the assumption that alternative media can be primarily understood as representing a disjuncture from the so-called status quo by presenting resources "antagonistic towards the mainstream and official channels" (Payne, 2014, p. 58). Taking issue with defining alternative media in terms of its so-called "oppositional" nature, they instead argue that such a characterization in fact, rarely exists "other than in the books of normative theorizing" (Payne, 2014, p. 59). Instead, they offer different ways of understanding alternative media. In one such notable attempt, Atton (2006) conceptualizes such media as potentially distinct from mainstream professional media along a spectrum that ranges from content or "subject matter" to the manner in which they are "organized" within specific "sociocultural contexts" (p. 10).

In other words, Atton's typology suggests that alternativeness can be variously manifest in relation to content and news values, forms of presentation, modes of distribution as well as what he terms "transformed social relations, roles and responsibilities," which involve changes in "notions of professionalism, competence and expertise" (p. 25) as well as "transformed communication processes" reflected in "horizontal linkages and networks" (p. 27). For this reason, Atton suggests that alternative media cannot be understood in terms of "consistent adherence to a pure fixed set of criteria," (p. 29) but instead should be defined by hybridity, as being different from the mainstream either in terms of products and processes or in some cases both. As he explains:

> Rather than attempt to define alternative media solely by content, I propose a theoretical and methodological framework that incorporates content as one element in an alternative media culture that is equally interested in the processes and relations that form around alternative media production. That is, I define alternative media as much by their capacity to generate non-standard, often infractory methods of creation, production and distribution. (p. 3)

Along similar lines, Bailey et al. (2008) have challenged "binaries" or what they deem to be an "unsustainable set of distinctions between commercial and non-commercial or radical and non-radical alternative media" (p. xii). Analyzing notions of alternative media embedded in so-called society-centric and relational perspectives, they argue that although alternative media have been variously conceptualized as "community media serving a local or dispersed community," as an "alternative to mainstream media," as a part of civil society or as a "rhizome," understood as an entity whose rules are constantly shifting, no single approach can be employed to understand such media. Instead they suggest "a panoptic approach," whereby alternative media are understood in terms of "diversity and multiplicity" (p. 150). As they put it:

> There exist distinct alternative media, some totally independent of market or government, some dependent on the state for their resources, others drawing on advertising to finance their operations, some re-producing hegemony, others clearly counter-hegemonic; some reactionary, some reformist, some revolutionary and others less obviously political. (p.153)

Meanwhile, Jeppesen (2016)—drawing on the varied conceptions of alternative media embedded in diverse theoretical approaches—identifies four distinct types of alternative media. These include: (i) "DIY media," influenced by connections to "left-leaning individualism," (ii) citizen and community-oriented participatory media informed by Marxist theories, (iii) critical media informed by the Frankfurt School that focus on the production of anti-capitalist content and finally (iv) autonomous/radical media which are influenced by social movement theories. These different types of alternative media, she argues, can be differentiated in terms of their "content, processes, and social movement actions," and analyzed on the basis of "their political ideologies," as well as who they claim to "empower" (p. 3). In her taxonomy, for instance, while DIY media are focused on the individual, community media, as their name suggests, aim to empower collectivities. For their part, critical media call for economic justice for the "post-industrial proletariat," while radical media's focus is on the collective organization of people (p. 16).

In a somewhat related fashion, Mowbray (2019) has argued that the various alternative media projects can be understood as being motivated by different "logics" (p. 23).[6] These range from: (i) participatory logics whereby alternative media primarily seek to provide opportunities for self-representation to marginalized groups and (ii) the logics of counter-public formation and facilitation where such media assist subordinated social groups in the construction of oppositional identities and discourses to (iii) media underpinned by critical-emancipatory logics that engage in "ideology critique" and provide "resources for counter-hegemonic struggles," as well as (iv) those defined by heterodox-creative logics that support the production of "culturally radical content" (p. 27). Based on this discussion, it is evident that scholars conceptualize alternative media encompassing not only different modes of expression and organization but also varied societal outcomes.

Although alternative media thus tend to be "multi-various in form, content and ethos," Harcup points out that "the scope of alternative journalism is more narrowly concerned with reporting/and or commenting on factual and topical events or current affairs" (2019). In other words, even though alternative journalism is undoubtedly embedded within the broad framework of alternative media, Harcup suggests that it constitutes a somewhat more specific category. In terms of usage, while the term has only relatively recently come to be widely employed (mainly in relation to the emergent underground press of the 1960s that emerged in countries such as Britain), the practices associated with alternative journalism are by no means new.

Indeed, "parallel forms" of journalism that involve the use of "journalistic techniques in the pursuit of alternative societal ends and/or use of different techniques for doing journalism itself" have existed in conjunction with journalism itself, emerging in "different ways, in different societies and in different eras" (Harcup, 2019). Thus, while some forms of alternative journalism include entities that engage in hybrid practices and combine both mainstream and alternative practices and modes of doing journalism, others seek to "to give the neglected their own means of communication," thus focusing on "playing a more consciously counter-hegemonic role within the public sphere" (Harcup, 2019). In the latter case, alternative journalism and its practitioners tend to be focused on "redressing and countering what they see as the failures of dominant media to adequately report certain issues, perspectives, or communities" (2019).

A similar range is manifest in the Indian context where alternative media outlets operating in digital spaces offering different types of journalism have become increasingly visible within the news landscape. These include independent, professional style newsrooms, various advocacy journalism-oriented outlets, rural citizen-based journalism entities engaged in hyperlocal coverage as well as news operations run entirely or primarily by women. These emergent web and social media-based entities are arguably "alternative"—in different ways and to different degrees—presenting contrasts to legacy media with regard to content, funding models, practice of journalism and adherence to professional norms as well as the extent to which they adopt a participatory approach defining "communication as a social rather than simply as an informational process" (Atton, 2006, p. 24).

In terms of practice, some digital alternative journalism outlets in India operate on the basis of occupational norms that closely approximate those associated with professional journalism—while also seeking to "fill informational or contextual gaps left by mainstream coverage" (Harcup, 2019). Many of these such as *The Scroll* or *The Wire* have been established by independent journalists who previously worked in commercial mainstream news outlets and either voluntarily left or were forced to quit such outlets under pressure from owners unwilling to challenge the government. These digital entities—while operating within the framework of professional journalism—nevertheless differ from commercial legacy media in the sense that they tend to emphasize different news values and avoid sensational or tabloid-style content while also containing more in-depth and investigative stories, including those that challenge establishment elites, notably members of the ruling BJP government as well as business leaders believed to be affiliated with the party.

Relatedly, other alternative journalism outlets stand out from traditional news organizations through their engagement with in-depth coverage of specific sets of concerns and issues rather than broad coverage of daily news. Significant among these is the People's Archive of Rural India (PARI) that seeks to explore issues of poverty, economic and social inequality and the effects of globalization, particularly as they affect the citizens of rural India. Still other outlets are defined by the explicit position-taking in their coverage. That is to say, these identity-based advocacy journalism organizations not only report on what they deem to be under-covered issues and groups but also offer alternative perspectives, draw on different sources and aim for greater involvement and participation by audiences, including in the processes of news production.

In doing so, they undertake what Schudson (2020) deems a very "useful" type of journalism because it "offers an interpretation of current events from an engaged stance that readers may find reinforcing or persuasive" (p. 15).

Focusing on these groups that tend to not only suffer from inadequate or unfair representation in news coverage but also lack what Fraser (1990) termed "parallel discursive arenas," these news media enable them to develop so-called "communities of interest" where community members can interact and engage with one another as well as develop counter-narratives that challenge mainstream representation. Through their emphasis on communicating the points of view of disadvantaged groups, these emergent digital outlets thus "deliberately and transparently stand for specific perspectives, with stories actively championing for certain ideas and values" (Cáceres, 2019). Typically, this is manifest in a critical perspective vis-a-vis exclusionary institutional structures and practices, especially those related to caste, gender or religion that continue to characterize Indian society.

The practices of such identity based, advocacy-oriented alternative news outlets thus constitute a significant contrast to legacy media outlets that have traditionally laid claim to legitimacy through their presumed adherence to the professional values of objectivity and neutrality, which are believed to be crucial to the occupational ideology or collective understanding of journalistic work (Deuze, 2005). And while these notions originally evolved in the context of Western journalism, many scholars have argued that globalization has led to "the adoption of similar journalistic norms and practices grounded in the normative ideals of professionalism" (Waisbord, p. 174). In the Indian context, even though news production tends to be driven by economic and political motivations (see for e.g., Chadha & Koliska, 2016; Jain et al., 2022) and journalists' adherence to professional values remains questionable, a commitment to objectivity and balance has been frequently highlighted as a defining quality by mainstream news organizations. Advocacy-oriented alternative journalism outlets on the other hand not only tend to disavow and challenge "objectivity and impartiality from both an ethical and practical standpoint" (Atton & Hamilton, 2008, p. 85) but also are often openly subjective in their coverage as part of a broader effort to counter what they perceive to be "dominant media's elite-oriented hierarchy of sources and viewpoints" (Hackett & Gurleyen, 2019, p. 56).

Outlets in this category of advocacy-oriented reporting include new and recently-established Dalit publications such as *National Dastak*, *Dalit Desk*, *Dalit Dastak* and *The Mooknayak* that focus on the concerns of low-caste groups who tend to be either erased or represented almost exclusively as victims of violence and poverty in mainstream news narratives. Meanwhile, outlets like *Maktoob Media*, *TwoCircles.net*, *Millat Times* and *Milli Gazette* that are aimed at Muslims not only seek to counter mainstream news coverage that "demonizes" the community but also offer "Muslim perspectives on developments" as well as "portray a world where Muslims are not always victims but a part of everyday Indian life" (Iyer, 2022). In other words, they seek primarily to give "voice" to a group that faces growing exclusion.

Meanwhile, other outlets like *Gram Vaani, CG Net Swara* and *Video Volunteers* distinguish themselves from mainstream media by emphasizing "wider social participation" in the "creation, production and dissemination" of news (Atton, 2006, p. 25). Focusing on hyperlocal rural coverage that is typically absent from traditional news accounts, they undertake news production through the establishment of participatory media platforms using mobile telephones to record audio and video. Thus, whereas traditional media outlets principally emphasize "informing" audiences, these entities privilege active involvement by the latter. In the process, they arguably give citizens access to the means of media production identified by Hamilton (2000) as a "crucial characteristic" of alternative media.

Also noteworthy among the category of alternative news outlets are those that foreground specific gender perspectives such as the rural news organization *Khabar Lahariya.* Run by an all-women newsroom of lower caste, Dalit and Muslim women, *Khabar Lahariya*'s journalists are drawn from the very rural communities that the outlet covers. But unlike mainstream news outlets that seek to define themselves as critical monitorial entities, *Khabar Lahariya* adopts an intersectional feminist approach in its coverage of the "stories of the injustices faced by women in different spheres of life as well as their successes" (Sinha & Malik, 2023). Using video, text and audio formats to produce and disseminate news across villages in parts of northern and central India, the outlet seeks to mobilize the affective proximity of rural women to their own contexts, training reporters and stringers in order to produce journalism based on nuanced and situated local knowledge.

The emergence of these varied types of digital alternative journalism has significantly altered India's news media terrain. Once a centralized, hierarchical structure where national and large regional mainstream print and television media outlets held exclusive sway over journalism across the country, it is now in a state of flux. For even as mainstream news organizations continue to play a major role in defining and articulating the public agenda, the news landscape is growing more fragmented due to the presence of new digital alternative journalism outlets that are motivated by varying missions and are often defined by different degrees of adherence to journalism's canonical professional values. The result is a fluid, decentralized and heterogeneous formation that merits investigation.

In the chapters that follow, I explore four different digital alternative news outlets through a series of empirically grounded essays. Although—as the discussion above indicates—digital alternative journalism outlets in India are manifest in different forms, I specifically investigate alternative news outlets that focus on communities facing marginalization, misrepresentation or erasure within mainstream media. As a whole, these individual outlets are connected in the sense that each one constitutes a "disruption" of the existing news media landscape, offering groups that are located outside the mainstream, new and unprecedented opportunities to express their own perspectives. Put differently, they represent efforts by subaltern groups to counter the "epistemic injustice" (Fricker, 2007) they routinely experience within mainstream media narratives and offer "alternatives" to India's hegemonic mainstream news media industry.

The data for these essays are derived from a combination of sources. I conducted over 50 semi-structured, in-depth interviews with journalists from different alternative journalism sites operating online. The interviews were conducted both in person as well as via Zoom or telephone. In some case, respondents have been identified, whereas in other cases the identities of individuals have been anonymized at their request. I also analyzed content samples from websites and YouTube channels, in addition to examining a variety of secondary data sources.

Following the first chapter (Introduction), Chapter 2 focuses on Dalit-produced media—manifest in the form of websites, Facebook pages and YouTube channels—that are aimed at members of India's low caste and tribal communities who represent the most under-privileged sections of Indian society. I argue in this chapter, that these news outlets which are aimed at developing a sense of identity while challenging and offering counter discourses to mainstream media narratives, contribute to the formation of a Dalit subaltern counterpublic.

In Chapter 3, I explore Muslim-produced news media which like Dalit media, also constitute a variant of advocacy media in that they "introduce alternative social actors…as the main subjects of their news and features" (Traber, 1985, p. 2). That is to say, they focus on grappling with the absence of voice both as process and as value (Couldry, 2010) experienced by their community in the context of the right-wing Hindu politics that currently permeates Indian polity. With this defining motivation, I explore their efforts to reclaim a sense of voice for members of the Muslim community who are increasingly confronted with state-sponsored exclusion and marginalization within Indian society.

In Chapter 4, I investigate developments related to citizen journalism in the Indian context. Following a brief discussion of the initial efflorescence of online citizen journalism as an urban phenomenon, I analyze the rural turn that it has taken in recent years. Examining various online citizen journalism projects that have emerged in rural communities across India, I suggest that although these projects which are mainly the result of collaborations between rural community members and professional journalists and NGOs, might not be "truly" bottom up in the sense of being organic, grassroots initiatives undertaken by "untrained, ordinary citizens" (Abbott, 2017), they are nevertheless significant. This is because they engage community members in participatory processes, offering them opportunities to become active citizens capable of seeking the redressal of their grievances and thereby potentially effecting change in their local environments.

In Chapter 5, I examine the emergence and workings of *Khabar Lahariya* or News Wave in the local dialect. KL—as it is often called—brands itself with the tag line "alternative and independent journalism by an all-women team of reporters from the Indian hinterland" and focuses on various types of rural coverage, including hyperlocal news that is absent from the mainstream news agenda. I explore how *Khabar Lahariya* seeks to fulfill its mission to provide locally relevant news while challenging "two of the most pervasive of social hierarchies" in India, namely "the gender and caste hierarchy" (Naqvi, 2007, p. 19), by the manner in which it undertakes its news production.

In a brief concluding end note, I reflect on the implications of the emergence of various forms of digital alternative journalism discussed in the preceding chapters for the Indian news media landscape.

Notes

1 The top six news sites in India belong to mainstream news outlets.
2 Over the past several years, owners of news outlets deemed opposed to prime minister Modi and his government have been targeted by government tax agencies and charged with a variety of financial crimes and irregularities.
3 In 2019, the Modi government prohibited government agencies from advertising in three major English-language dailies—*The Telegraph, Times of India*, and *The Hindu*—but while it provided no reason for its decision, media commentators have suggested that the action was "retaliation" for critical coverage (Ghoshal, 2019). Additionally, in 2019, the government withheld advertising from three leading newspapers in Kashmir in response to a so-called "anti-India" tone in their coverage (International Federation of Journalists, 2019).
4 While originally the term alternative news media was mainly used to denote progressive counter-hegemonic media that challenged mainstream media institutions, recently, the term has been increasingly employed to characterize a variety of hyperpartisan outlets that have emerged in conjunction with right-wing populist movements and position themselves corrective of mainstream news media (Holt et al., 2019).
5 Although the internet—which initially came to India in 1986 in the form of the Educational Research Network (ERNET) aimed primarily at those involved in educational or research activities—was introduced as a commercial service in select metropolitan cities, in the mid-1990s, its initial growth was slow. The situation changed in the 2000s when the Indian government introduced new broadband policies and cheap smartphones and low-cost data services became widely available in India.
6 However, Mowbray does acknowledge that in practice these so-called "logics," in practice often "shade" into one another" (p. 23).

References

Abbott, J. Y. (2017). Tensions in the scholarship on participatory journalism and citizen journalism. *Annals of the International Communication Association, 41*(3–4), 278–297.

Atton, C. (2006). *Alternative media*. Sage.

Atton, C. (2010). Alternative journalism: Ideology and practice. In S. Allan (Ed.), *Routledge companion to news and journalism* (pp. 169–178). Routledge.

Atton, C., & Hamilton, J. (2008). *Alternative journalism*. Sage.

Bailey, O. G., Cammaerts, B., & Carpentier, N. (2008). *Understanding alternative media.* McGraw Hill.

Bajpai, P. P. (2018, July 8). Exclusive: Punya Prasun Bajpai reveals the story of his exit from ABP News. The Wire. https://thewire.in/media/punya-prasun-bajpai-abp-news-narendra-modi

Basuroy, T. (2022). Mobile phone internet user penetration in India from 2010 to 2020, with estimates until 2040. *Statista.* https://www.statista.com/statistics/309019/india-mobile-phone-internet-user-penetration/

Bidwai, P. (2011). The growing crisis of credibility of the Indian media. Transnational Institute. https://www.efsas.org/commentaries/wayward-sections-of-the-indianmedia-harming-the-country-interests-and-its-image-abroad/

Cáceres, I. B. (2019). Advocacy journalism. Oxford Communication Research Encyclopedias. https://doi.org/10.1093/acrefore/9780190228613.013.776

Chadha, K. (2017). The Indian news media industry: Structural trends and journalistic implications. *Global Media and Communication, 13*(2), 139–156.

Chadha, K. (2019). Media stings and the normalization of scandal in India. In H. Tumber, & S. Waisbord (Eds.), *Routledge companion to media and scandal* (pp. 236–244). Routledge.

Chadha, K., & Arya, S. (2021). Challenges to press freedom in India. Oxford Communication Research Encyclopedias. https://doi.org/10.1093/acrefore/9780190228613.013.974

Chadha, K., & Koliska, M. (2016). Playing by a different set of rules: Journalistic values in India's regional television newsrooms. *Journalism Practice, 10*, 608–625.

Comedia (1984). The alternative press; The development of underdevelopment. *Media, Culture and Society, 6*, 95–102.

Couldry, N. (2010). *Why voice matters.* Sage Publications.

Deuze, M. (2005). What is journalism? Professional identity and ideology of journalists reconsidered. *Journalism, 6*(4), 442–464.

Doron, A., & Jeffrey, R. (2013). *The great Indian phone book. How the cheap cell phone changes business, politics, and daily life.* Harvard University Press.

Downing, J. (2001). *Radical media: Rebellious communication and social movements.* Sage.

Franklin, B. (1997). *Newszak and news media.* Hodder Education Publishers.

Fraser, N. (1990). Rethinking the public sphere. *Social Text, 25/26*, 56–80.

Fricker, M. (2007). *Epistemic injustice. Power and the ethics of knowing.* Oxford University Press.

Fuchs, C. (2011). *Foundations of critical media and information studies.* Routledge.

Ghoshal, D. (2019, June 28). Modi government freezes ads in three newspapers. *Reuters.* https://www.reuters.com/article/india-media-idINKCN1TT1R6

Gopalakrishnan, R. (2018, April 26). Indian journalists say they are intimidated, ostracized if they criticize Modi and the BJP. *Reuters.* https://www.reuters.com/article/us-india-politics-media-analysis/indian-journalists-say-they-intimidated-ostracized-if-they-criticize-modi-and-the-bjp-idUSKBN1HX1F4

Hackett, R. A., & Gurleyen, P. (2019). Beyond the binaries? Alternative journalism and objective journalism. In C. Atton (Ed.), *The Routledge companion to alternative and community media* (pp. 54–65). Routledge.

Hallin, D., & Mancini, P. (1994). *Comparing media systems.* Cambridge University Press.

Hamilton, J. (2000). Alternative media: Conceptual difficulties, critical possibilities. *Journal of Communication Inquiry, 24*(4), 357–378.

Harcup, T. (2019). Alternative journalism. In J.F. Nussbaum (Ed.), *Oxford Research Encyclopedia of Communication*. Oxford University Press. https://oxfordre.com/communication/display/10.1093/acrefore/9780190228613.001.0001/acrefore-9780190228613-e-780?d=%2F10.1093%2Facrefore%2F9780190228613.001.0001%2Facrefore-9780190228613-e-780&p=emailAWzyKly00HHgU

Holt, K., Figenschou, T. U., & Frischlich, L. (2019). Key dimensions of alternative news media. *Digital Journalism, 7*(7), 860–869.

International Federation of Journalists (2019). South Asia Press Freedom Report 2018–2019. https://samsn.ifj.org/wp-content/uploads/2019/05/IFJ_PF_Report_2019_LR_spread.pdf

Iyer, A. (2022, October 29). As Hindutva has grown, so have websites reporting on India's embattled Muslims. *Scroll*. https://scroll.in/article/1035586/as-hindutva-has-grown-in-india-so-have-websites-reporting-on-the-plight-of-embattled-muslims

Jain, S. (2015). India: Multiple media explosions. In K. Nordenstreng, & D. K. Thussu (Eds.), *Mapping BRICS media* (pp. 145–164). Routledge.

Jain, G., Suman, S., Gupta, S., & Tiwari, A. A. (2022). Media bias and Bollywood: An untold story. In I. Qureshi, B. Bhatt, S. Gupta, & A. A. Tiwari (Eds.), *Causes and symptoms of socio-cultural polarization: Role of information and communication technologies* (pp. 211–232). Springer.

Jeffrey, R. (2000). *India's newspaper revolution: Capitalism, politics and the Indian language press, 1977-99. Oxford University Press.*

Jeppesen, S. (2016). Understanding alternative media power: Mapping content & practice to theory, ideology, and political action. *Democratic Communique, 27*(1). https://doi.org/10.7275/democratic-communique.185

Joseph, M. (2002, July 6). *Indian government targeting portal. Wired*. https://www.wired.com/2002/07/indian-govt-targeting-portal/

Kant, R. (2019, December 3). Indian economy headed for structural breakdown. *Asia Times*. https://asiatimes.com/2019/12/india-economy-slowdown-demonetization-gst/

Khanna, N. (2022, August 16). Digital and alternate media is slowly displacing the legacy Indian print media. *Indian Printer and Publisher*. https://indianprinterpublisher.com/blog/2022/08/digital-and-alternate-media-is-slowly-displacing-the-legacy-indian-print-media/

Krishnan, A. (2021). India. Digital News Report 2021. Reuters Institute, Oxford University. https://reutersinstitute.politics.ox.ac.uk/digital-news-report/2021/india

Krishnan, A. (2023). India. News Report 2023. Reuters Institute, Oxford University. https://reutersinstitute.politics.ox.ac.uk/digital-news-report/2023/india

Mahajan, D. (2004, August 1). Advertorials: Blurring the dividing line. *India Together*. https://indiatogether.org/advert-media

Maheshwari, S., & Sparks, C. (2018). Political elites and journalistic practices in India: A case of institutionalized heteronomy. *Journalism, 13*(2), 231–247.

Mazumdar, A. (2016). Paid news in India disrupts press freedom and ethical conduct. *International Communication Research Journal, 51*(2), 43–67.

Mohan, J. (2021, June 28). Media bias and democracy in India. South Asian Voices https://southasianvoices.org/media-bias-and-democracy-in-india/#easy-footnote-bottom-1-14657

Mowbray, M. (2019). Alternative logics? Parsing the literature on alternative media. In C. Atton (Ed.), *The Routledge companion to alternative and community media* (pp. 21–31). Routledge.

Mudgal, V. (2011). Rural coverage in Hindi and English dailies. *Economic & Political Weekly, 46*(35), 92–97.

Naqvi, F. (2007). *Waves in the hinterland.* Nirantar Foundation.

NewsLaundry (2022). Gender representation in Indian newsrooms. https://www.themediarumble.com/reports

Ninan, S. (2019, July 5). How India's news media have changed since 2014: Greater self-censorship, dogged digital resistance. *Scroll.In.* https://scroll.in/article/929461/greater-self-censorship-dogged-digital-resistance-how-indias-news-media-have-changed-since-2014

Outlook Web Desk (2022, February 4). Who owns the news and why? *Outlook.* https://www.outlookindia.com/website/story/who-owns-the-news-and-why/294350

Oxfam India-NewsLaundry (2022). *Who tells our stories matters. Caste Representation Report.* https://www.themediarumble.com/reports

Payne, J. G. (2014). Feminist media as alternative media? Feminist media from the perspective of alternative media studies. In E. Zobl and R. Drueke (Eds.). *Feminist media: Participatory spaces, networks, and cultural citizenship* (pp. 55–72). Bielefeld.

Press Council of India (2010). Draft report on paid news. https://dl.icdst.org/pdfs/files4/31ef62e00fdd670c947410f210361b5d.pdf

Pulla, P. (2020, May 14). When an article disappears, we have more than just a pandemic to worry about. *The Wire.* https://thewire.in/health/india-media-coronavirus-government

Reporters without Borders (2018). Media ownership monitor: Who owns the media in India. https://rsf.org/en/media-ownership-monitor-who-owns-media-india

Sam, C. (2019, June 3). Media pluralism under threat. *NewsClick.* https://www.newsclick.in/Media-Pluralism-India-Under-Threat-RSF-Reporters-Without-Border

Schudson, M. (2020). *Journalism. Why it matters.* Polity Press.

Sharma, A. (2013). In need of a Leveson? Journalism in India in times of paid news and private treaties. Reuters Institute, Oxford University. https://reutersinstitute.politics.ox.ac.uk/our-research/need-leveson-journalism-india-times-paid-news-and-private-treaties

Sharma, S. (2019, December 7). Why is the Indian media almost blind to gender issues? And how can this be rectified? *NewsLaundry.* https://www.newslaundry.com/2019/12/07/why-is-the-indian-media-almost-blind-to-gender-issues-and-how-can-this-be-rectified

Sinha, A., & Malik, K. M. (2023). Women journalists of Khabar Lahariya and Namaskar: Enabling gendered media ecology in rural India. In A. Kaushik & A. Suchang (eds.) *Narratives and new voices from India* (pp.). Springer.

Sodhi, T. (2023, May 5). At least 44 times over 5 years: The NIA, ED and I-T 'crackdown' on the media. *NewsLaundry.* https://www.newslaundry.com/2023/05/05/at-least-44-times-over-5-years-the-nia-ed-and-i-t-crackdown-on-the-media

Streitmatter, R. (2001). *Voices of revolution: The dissident press in America.* Columbia University Press.

Thomas, P. (2010). *Political economy of communications in India: The good, the bad and the ugly.* Sage.

Thussu, D. K. (2007). *News as entertainment: The rise of global infotainment.* Sage.

Traber, M. (1985). *Alternative journalism, alternative media.* World Association for Christian Communication.

Vengattil, M. (2022, March 1). India's Adani makes foray into media business with Quintillion stake. *Reuters.* https://www.reuters.com/world/india/indias-adani-makes-foray-into-media-business-with-quintillion-stake-2022-03-01/

Waltz, M. (2005). *Alternative and activist media.* Edinburgh University Press.

2 Digital Dalit News Outlets
Alternative Spaces Facilitating Counterpublic Formation?

Background

On January 17, 2016, Rohith Vemula, a 26-year old, Dalit PhD student at the Hyderabad Central University in southern India, committed suicide by hanging himself from a ceiling fan in his friend's hostel room. Meaning "broken" or "scattered," the term Dalit refers to individuals who are held to be outside the four-fold division of India's caste system,[1] and hence located at the very bottom of India's social hierarchy. In the months prior to this event, Mr. Vemula—along with four other Dalit students—had been denied fellowship funds and prevented from entering university-provided housing by authorities. These punitive actions stemmed from a complaint that he and the other students had assaulted a leader of the *Akhil Bharatiya Vidyarthi Parishad* (ABVP), the student-wing of the ruling Hindu-nationalist *Bharatiya Janata Party*, traditionally associated with upper caste Hindus. Mr. Vemula and his companions denied the charge, arguing that they had been targeted for their involvement in efforts to counter casteism at the university through the Ambedkar Students Association, a Dalit student organization. In December 2015, the university made a final recommendation to expel Mr. Vemula. A month later he killed himself, leaving behind a searing note blaming "the system" for his death (*The Wire* Staff, 2019).

Predictably, this event initially received little attention from the mainstream media which remained stuck in the first stage of what has been termed the "four-stage lifecycle of coverage," as it relates to Dalits, namely "indifference, sensationalism, accusations and victim-blaming" (Shinde, 2020). But while mainstream news coverage of Mr. Vemula's suicide and the Dalit student protests that followed was limited, the story was kept alive by a handful of Dalit-run digital outlets that were engaged in producing news and commentary on issues and events related to their community. Notable among these were *Roundtable India* and especially the YouTube channel and website *Dalit Camera*. Founded in 2012 with the goal of documenting "the voices of Dalits, Adivasis, Bahujans, and minorities" (Mohammed, 2020), *Dalit Camera* provided intense, unedited coverage of the protests as well as deeply personal, first-person accounts from

DOI: 10.4324/9781003244202-2

Dalit students detailing the caste-based discrimination that they routinely faced in educational institutions (Paul & Dowling, 2018).

The Vemula case was not the only instance in which Dalit news outlets played a critical role. More recently, Dalit-produced media have been similarly instrumental in drawing public attention to what *eventually* came to be known as the notorious Hathras gang rape case that occurred in September 2020. In this case, four upper caste men were accused of brutally raping a 19-year old rural Dalit woman in the northern Indian state of Uttar Pradesh. While mainstream news organizations did not cover the issue until the death of the young woman from injuries sustained during the assault, Dalit journalists not only highlighted the crime from the outset but also contextualized the event in relation to endemic issues of caste-based violence (Shinde, 2020).

In recent years, such advocacy-oriented digital entities that define themselves as explicitly focused on Dalit communities have emerged as a significant and increasingly visible form of alternative journalism in the Indian context (Paul & Dowling, 2018). And although no reliable census of such outlets exists, it is estimated there are over 150 Dalit-produced news sources operating in India in a variety of languages (Sharma, 2020). Especially prominent among these are several YouTube news channels. According to Dalit scholar and media observer, Dilip Mandal, many of these channels have significant audiences. The largest among these (see Table 2.1) are *National Dastak* (3.5 million subscribers), *Bahujan TV* (2 million subscribers) and *National India News* (2 million subscribers). Other popular YouTube channels include *Awaaz India TV*, *Mulnivasi TV* (MNTV), *Samta Awaz TV*, *Dalit News*

Table 2.1 YouTube channels posting on Dalit Issues

Name	Subscribers in 100 thousands	Year of establishment
National Dastak	50.42	2015
Bahujan TV	20.67	2015
National India News	20.4	2017
Awaaz India TV	10.48	2013
Dalit Dastak	8.89	2012
SM News	7.58	2015
Dalit News Network	7.24	2017
Mulnivasi TV (MNTV)	6.09	2015
Bahujan Hub	2.27	2016
Dalit Camera	0.82	2012
Dalit Song	0.43	2010
Jai Bhim Channel	0.25	2016
The Think	0.21	2020
The News Beak	4.74	2018
Dalit Times	NA	2021
Forward Press	0.19	2012

Source: Kumar (2021).

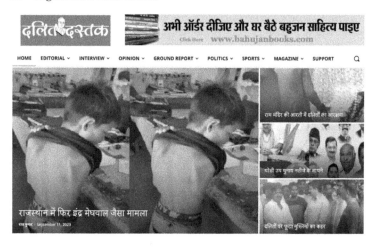

Figure 2.1 Screenshot from the *Dalit Dastak* website, showing the image of a Dalit boy who had been beaten by a teacher for drinking water from a container meant for upper castes. The story also references a prior, similar case that resulted in the death of a student.

Network (DNN), *SM News* and *Voice News Network* as well as those channels run by individual vloggers like Activist Ved (Mandal, 2020).

Some Dalit-focused digital news entities such as *Forward Press, Roundtable India* and *Justice News* operate exclusively as websites while yet others combine a website presence with YouTube channels such as the *Dalit Dastak, Dalit Desk, National Dastak, The Shudra* and *The Mooknayak*. These outlets also vary in their coverage focus. While many like *Dalit Dastak* and *The Shudra* (see Figures 2.1 and 2.2), have a national focus. Others like *Nishpaksh Divya Sandesh* operate as a regional Hindi daily in India's most populous state, Uttar Pradesh.

Financially, while some outlets such as *The Newsbeak* and *Dalit Dastak* have been able to monetize their content by obtaining advertising through YouTube and Facebook, others such as *Dalit Desk* and *The Mooknayak* rely primarily on crowdfunding campaigns from their readers, often in the form of small donations. Recounting the story of a daily wage worker who contributed to *The Mooknayak*, the site's founder Meena Kotwal recently said that many of those supporting her outlet were manual workers who sent "sums like fifty or hundred rupees ($0.62-$1) because that is all they could manage," but that they did so since they wanted to support an outlet that carried their stories (Agarwal, 2022). In terms of content, whereas some of these alternative outlets offer original reporting, others mainly focus on providing commentary and opinions on news events as well as "thematic" perspectives on problems faced by Dalit communities. Together, they thus seek to "offer a response and counterview to the cartelized hegemony of the English news," (Bhim, 2018, quoted in Paul &

Figure 2.2 Screenshot from *The Shudra* website detailing a Dalit youth's journey across India to raise awareness about challenges faced by his community.

Dowling, 2018, p. 1240) while also—in the words of Dalit journalist Meena Kotwal—striving to "politicize and visibilize" issues related to Dalits that fail to receive adequate coverage in the mainstream media (Agarwal, 2022).

Dalits in Indian Society and Media: Background and Contemporary Developments

As a subaltern community, Dalits have long experienced exclusion and discrimination in the context of the Indian caste system, which is made up of three upper castes (Brahmins, Kshatriyas and Vaisyas) and a fourth lower caste of Sudras who face varying degrees of economic and social discrimination. But unlike Sudras who are included in the caste hierarchy, Dalits who include a variety of different castes are considered to be outside it, deemed "untouchable," for their involvement in occupations such as leather work and scavenging that are considered ritually "impure," in the Hindu social order. In other words, Dalit—a term that has no actual legal standing[2]—represents an "umbrella term" that "refers to traditionally outcaste groups…in the stratified and hierarchical Hindu caste system, which also includes members of other faiths such as Sikhism and Islam (Thakur, 2019, p. 344). But even though Dalits thus constitute a heterogeneous group, who are varied in terms of their geographic locations, political affiliations, languages and religions (Thakur, 2019), as a category, they are nevertheless united by the fact that they have been consistently oppressed in the context of the caste system that underpins Hindu society. For example, Dalits have traditionally been prevented by members of the upper castes from entering public spaces such as schools and temples, confined to living within specific localities and denied the opportunity to enter high status occupations (Thapa et al., 2021). Consequently, their access to the media has been quite limited.

Speaking historically, early efforts to challenge the caste system occurred in the 16th century, but until the first half of the 19th century, protests against Brahmanical domination were "mainly expressed in religious idioms" by contemporary Hindu reformers (Harshvardhan & Mogha, 2022). Modern initiatives involving the use of advocacy media outlets to counter caste-based discrimination and help Dalits develop an alternative identity only emerged in the late 19th century. Significant among these outlets was the weekly Marathi-language newspaper *Dinbandhu* (Friend of the Poor) associated with the anti-caste movement established by Jyotiba Phule in western India. Established in 1877, the publication focused specifically on the issues and concerns of so-called "untouchable" communities (Kidambi, 2016). By the late 1920s, various types of publications that highlighted Dalit concerns and played a vital role in mobilizing support for anti-caste perspectives and politics had emerged resulting in the growth of Dalit mass movements in different parts of the country.

For example, in northern India, Swami Achutanand established a fortnightly newspaper *Adi-Hindu* which ran from 1924 to 1934. Similarly, in the present-day western state of Maharashtra, Dalit leader Dr. B.R. Ambedkar—who led numerous Dalit agitations aimed at attacking the caste-based Hindu social order—published a variety of publications, including Marathi-language papers such as *Mooknayak* (Leader of the Voiceless) and *Bahishkrit Bharat* (Excluded India) as well as the fortnightly *Janata* (People). Meanwhile, in southern India, E.V. Ramaswamy Naicker who launched the so-called self-respect movement that demanded equal rights for members of the lowest strata of Indian society launched Tamil-language outlets such as the weekly newspaper *Kudi Arasu* (Rule of the People) and *Viduthalai* (Liberation).

These outlets set themselves apart from the mainstream media, including the nationalist press, which Dalit leaders perceived as dominated by upper castes and unwilling to represent their communities. Emphasizing this point, Ambedkar observed:

> Throughout India, each day our people are suffering under authoritarianism with no consideration, and discrimination; those are not covered in the newspapers. By a planned conspiracy the newspapers are involved full-fledged in silencing our views on socio-political problems.
>
> (Ambedkar, 1993)

From the very outset, Dalit outlets hence positioned themselves as explicit advocates for the rights of their people, taking "bold positions on several contentious issues pertaining to religion, society and politics" (Ratnamala, 2012). Indeed, throughout the course of India's anti-colonial movement, Dalit newspapers and magazines questioned the nationalist political movement and its press's "indifference to the question of caste" (Pol, 2018).

These tensions persisted in the post-colonial context even as the Indian government "postulated the idea of the Indian state as an inclusive space of casteless and secular citizens" (Rawat & Satyanarayana, 2016) and banned caste-related discrimination in 1950 as part of the new constitution. However, Dalits (officially classified as Scheduled Castes and Scheduled Tribes according to India's new constitution)[3] continued to face exclusion both in society and in the news media. Responding to ongoing marginalization, the 1970s witnessed a resurgence of Dalit activism as the Dalit Panthers—inspired by the US-based Black Panther movement—launched a series of political movements that were accompanied by a revival of Dalit publications in the form of literary magazines across Western India. These vernacular language publications defined themselves as "resisting the establishment," and interrogating the status quo represented by mainstream socio-political and media discourse (Oza, 2019, p. 405).

Around the same time, in northern India, Kanshi Ram—who established the *Bahujan Samaj Party* aimed at advancing the interests of oppressed castes in India—underscored the need for "a parallel media for the mass Bahujan movement." To this end, he established multiple media outlets, including monthlies such as *The Oppressed Indian* and the monthly *Bahujan Sangathak*, writing that "people of the backward and minority communities, who form about 85% of India's population, have little share in the news service of the nation. News regarding them or pertaining to their pressing problems appears in the press in a casual manner… the caste Hindu monopoly of the press gives only sketchy news about the outrages and the atrocities committed on the oppressed Indians" (Banik, 2016). Such publications met at least a "minimal definition of alternative media," as a form of media "which challenges at least implicitly, actual concentrations of media power" (Curran & Couldry, 2003,

p. 7). But despite the presence of such print-based alternative news outlets, Dalit-produced print media remained limited both in their reach and in their ability to develop an audience during much of the 20th century.

Meanwhile, Dalit journalists also continued to experience exclusion and marginalization. In fact, even though discrimination based on caste was deemed illegal in post-independence India and a so-called "reservation" system for Dalits was implemented in political office, government jobs and educational institutions, such affirmative action did not extend to the private sector, which encompassed the majority of the media industry. Consequently, even though "Dalit and Adivasi journalists graduated from journalism institutes," they "failed to get jobs" (Srivastava, 2022). For instance, an analysis of 700 accredited journalists based in New Delhi—the capital and political center of India—conducted in 1996 by journalist B.N. Uniyal,[4] found no Dalits in the group at all (Uniyal, 1996). Similarly, Robin Jeffrey's analysis of the post-liberalization growth of India's newspaper industry found that "although Dalits numbered close to 150 million people in the 1990s, almost none worked on daily newspapers as reporters or sub-editors. There were no Dalit editors and no Dalit-run dailies. Dalit periodicals where they existed were fringe publications, often with a literary emphasis and with limited influence beyond the circle that produced them" (2001, p. 225).

A subsequent 2006 study, by New Delhi-based think tank Center for the Study of Developing Societies, which examined the backgrounds of top editors across 37 leading English and Hindi language newspapers and television channels, found that of the 315 key editorial leaders surveyed, almost 90% of the decision-makers in the English language print media and 79% in television were found to belong to the so-called "upper castes" (Yadav et al., 2006). The study also found that 49% of newsroom leaders were Brahmins who make up approximately 4% of the population. There were no Dalits in the newsrooms surveyed and only 4% of newsworkers belonged to castes designated as Shudras (Yadav et al., 2006). More recently, a 2019 survey analyzing the social backgrounds (i.e. caste) of TV anchors, panelists, and bylined journalists across various forms of media found that "of the 218 persons occupying 'leadership positions' across various media types, 88 percent come from upper-caste Hindus," and that if magazines and digital media were excluded from the analysis, "the share of marginalized groups in the leadership of English and Hindi newspapers and TV channels is exactly zero" (Yadav, 2022). In this regard, the contemporary state of Indian news media vis-a-vis marginalized groups arguably parallels the American press of the 1960s, which according to the Kerner Commission ignored African American perspectives and saw the world "with white men's eyes and white perspective" (1968, p. 213).

Moreover, even in cases when Dalit journalists were hired by mainstream news organizations, they found themselves confronting significant structural barriers paralleling those faced by minority journalists in the Global North.

These included being limited to covering issues related to their social identity as well as lack of access to networks and professional development opportunities within newsrooms (Agarwal, 2022; Harad, 2020). Commenting on the "lack of social capital" experienced by members of his community, a Dalit journalist said that "he felt that he lacked a certain network or ability to form a network, which can be helpful in sourcing stories, getting fellowships and generally moving up the ladder" (Harad, 2020). Dalit reporters also referenced routinized ostracism and harassment by upper caste colleagues (Balasubramaniam, 2011). In this regard, a female journalist and news portal founder said that casteism even pervaded the newsrooms of international news organizations such as the BBC, citing her own negative experiences while working there (Agarwal, 2022).

Predictably, this absence of Dalit journalists (both in the ranks and especially at the editorial levels where coverage decisions are made) has profound consequences for the nature of reportage. For example, even though Dalits, who number over 230 million out of a total population of 1.4 billion in India (Subramanyam, 2020), constitute one of the largest marginalized groups in the world (Dowling, 2020) and experience high levels of poverty,[5] as well as caste-based exclusion and violence especially in rural areas, they receive limited coverage (Achanta, 2015). In this regard, a study published by Oxfam India and media watchdog group *Newslaundry* in 2019 found that of the 972 cover stories carried by leading Indian magazines, only ten were related to issues of caste. The study also found that a single newspaper (*Indian Express*) accounted for more than half of the coverage on caste-related issues among English-languages newspapers (Bhatia et al., 2019).

In addition to contributing to the symbolic annihilation of Dalit communities, their concerns and perspectives, the lack of Dalit journalists in mainstream news outlets also affects the nature of coverage when communities *are* reported upon. Commenting on mainstream approaches to the coverage of his community, a Dalit journalist pointed out that journalists' understanding of what was "on trend" or "necessary" tended to be shaped by their identity as "upper-caste urbanites" and reflected their lack of awareness of other, especially rural realities. Similarly, another Dalit journalist—who had been employed at a leading Hindi language paper—found that stories he wrote based on information from Dalit organizations rarely made it into the newspaper. Recalling his experience, he said, "I was getting a lot of news about Dalits…the desk was killing my stories and if I asked them why they weren't publishing my articles day after day, they would say I shouldn't complain as long as I was being paid a salary." When he protested, he was told "kranti nahin karni hai. Naukri karo (Don't start a revolution; do your job)." Eventually, he left his job because as he put it, "My whole purpose was to highlight the voices of my people in the media" (Poonam & Bansal, 2023).

On parallel lines, a former broadcast journalist said that when he tried to get his mainstream television news channel to cover a 2016 lynching of Dalit men by upper caste Hindus in the state of Gujarat, his editor dismissed him saying "your show is in the evening when people have come home and are drinking their tea after work, they don't want to see such things." Instead, he said, he found himself covering "stories like one about monkeys ringing bells in temples, because it offered entertaining visuals," leading him to ask "what the f*** am I doing here when my people are suffering." Indeed, as Paul and Dowling (2018) accurately suggest though "caste discrimination has been a staple of Indian society for centuries, the specific manifestations of oppression rarely make headlines in the mainstream news media, which are owned and operated primarily by upper-caste Hindus" (p. 1239).

And even when such "manifestations of oppression" are reported through the coverage of "passionate episodes involving conflict and violence associated with caste" (Fonseca et al., 2019), these tend to be usually written by upper caste journalists who make up a majority of those writing on issues related to caste in Hindi and English newspapers. Such "monotonic" coverage is problematic for a variety of reasons. For one, urban journalists who "parachute" into rural communities tend to treat members of the Dalit caste as "objects" to be reported upon. Moreover, because coverage locates Dalits almost exclusively in negative contexts, they appear as "the source of trouble and problems" (Fonseca et al., 2019). In other words, news media convey the message that Dalits are "poor, naive, ignorant, victims, and sometimes perpetrators of violence" (Jeffrey, 2001) while offering no insight "into the multitude of aspects necessarily present in the life of the lower caste population" (Fonseca et al., 2019).

Such coverage of Dalits whereby they are either erased or misrepresented not only results in the legitimization of upper caste perspectives within the public sphere but arguably undermines democratic governance itself. But whereas in the past, Dalit communities were limited in their ability to challenge mainstream narratives, growing access to digital technologies has facilitated communicative opportunities for at least some segments of this disenfranchised group (Ahuja, 2018). Thus, whereas Spivak (1988) in response to her own rhetorical question "can the subaltern speak?" asserted that a lack of political power and epistemic capital rendered subordinated groups voiceless, this situation is beginning to shift, at least to some degree. As Mitra (2004) has argued the Internet has afforded "dispossessed groups," a venue to "produce their presence" (p. 496). Indeed, growing access to cheap cell phones and ubiquitous mobile internet services, combined with the growth of an educated Dalit middle class (Jaffrelot, 2016) and the emergence of Dalit political movements in response to events such as the Vemula suicide[6] (Pai, 2020), have enabled some Dalits to enter the public domain. Employing "digital tools to narrate their oppressive past," (Paul & Dowling, 2018, p. 1), many have also established their own news media outlets. As Thirumal and Tartikov (2011) express it:

> A small but vigorous group of Dalits are using information technologies to transcend barriers of caste in ways not possible before, and thus to take advantage of democratic opportunities that can lead to breaking through caste and the ritual walls to share understandings and interests with each other…more importantly Dalits have found a means of communicating with each other beyond the control of others. (p. 22)

Making this point in relation to the media, Dalit journalist and activist Meena Kandasamy writes:

> Big media house which own the major publications rarely give opportunity to Dalit (ex-untouchable) writers, and there's an absence of Dalit/anti-caste writers who write in English. The elitist writers want to write the feel-good stuff, India Shining myths, and that's the work that gets into print. So, I wanted to tap the power and enormous outreach of the internet: how anyone can write and be read/heard in the virtual space. I was not writing because anyone was commissioning me, I didn't have to follow other people's diktats, I could speak my mind. Google and tagging ensure that I can get heard without having my own column in any newspaper. Sometimes it helped me bring some happenings to light—such as the recent inside story of Dalit students being beaten up at a law university in Chennai (the mainstream media merely reported it as a—clash at first.
> (quoted in Kumar & Subramani, 2014)

Reflecting similar sentiments, a journalist who had worked in mainstream newsrooms and now affiliated with *The Shudra*, a recently established Dalit news portal—whose name represents an attempt to re-appropriate a term sometimes used as a slur—commented that:

> Traditional media such as a satellite television channel or a newspaper all required large capital investment and were not feasible for Dalit communities but online media, especially social media platforms, have been a boon because all that is needed is a phone with a decent camera and a mobile internet connection, this makes it easy for community members to access and share relevant content for which there is a real hunger.

In interviews, many other Dalit journalists also pointed out that growing rural access to smartphones enabled members of Dalit communities not only to act as witnesses but also to share their videos with Dalit journalists and news platforms who later pursued these stories, often turning them viral and thereby "forcing" mainstream news outlets to cover them in an act of (limited) agenda setting. Several other leading Dalit journalists also underscored the role of technology in enabling them to build upon the existing legacy of Ambedkarite journalism, asserting that digital media had lowered previously insurmountable barriers to entry and made it possible for them to produce and disseminate news about their communities in an unprecedented manner. As the editor of *Dalit Desk*, a crowdfunded news website that defines its mission as "providing a loud mouth to unheard voices," said:

> We have always had a tradition of our own outlets and journalism but it was limited by a lack of resources, now it is not.

Discursive Practices of Contemporary Dalit-Produced Digital Journalism

In terms of content, digital Dalit journalism outlets seek to produce and amplify "forms of 'recognition' to regions and minorities," while also providing venues for oppositional subordinated voices (Dowling, 2020, p. 88) who lack access to and representation within India's public sphere. In other words, these alternative journalism outlets arguably serve as what Fraser (1990) identified as "parallel discursive arenas" for members of the Dalit community. In her critique of Habermas's theory of the bourgeois public sphere, Fraser has argued that the conceptualization of the public sphere as a space in which private citizens come together to "deliberate as peers" and engage in "unrestricted rational discussion of public matters" (p. 59) did not account for the fact that it was impossible to "bracket" existing social inequalities within stratified societies. As a result, even when individuals were legally guaranteed similar access into the discursive arena represented by the public sphere, their ability to participate on an equal footing was impacted by ascriptive markers of race, class and gender. Certainly, this would appear to be the case in India where numerous such barriers, such as caste, result in the exclusion of indigenous groups from the Indian public sphere (Chandoke, 2005).

For this reason, Fraser argues that traditionally disenfranchised social communities have often found it "advantageous to constitute alternative publics" operating outside the dominant public sphere where they could "successfully critique the dominant society," (Fraser, 1990, p. 67) without being subject to surveillance by powerful societal entities. More specifically, she has suggested that secure in these spaces, subaltern groups can "invent and circulate counter-discourses which in turn permit them to formulate oppositional interpretations of their own identities, interests and needs," (p. 67) "free of the supervision of dominant groups," and thus find "the right voice or words to express their thoughts" (p. 66). In other words, such spaces offer marginalized communities the opportunity to "influence and challenge dominant discourses, foregrounding their experiences and projecting their voices" (Suk et al., 2023). An analysis of the content of leading English and Hindi Dalit-produced digital news outlets, alongside interviews with Dalit journalists, indicates that such venues increasingly operate as alternative spaces of the type that Fraser and others theorizing counterpublics conceptualize.

In these online venues, Dalits challenge mainstream or what many called "Manuvadi" or "Manustream" news media (referencing the ancient Indian lawgiver Manu whose writings codified the principles upholding the hierarchical caste system[7]) through a variety of discursive practices. And operating as such, they come together to facilitate the formation—at least to some degree—what Fraser (1990) identifies as a subaltern counterpublic. One such key discursive practice is the effort by online Dalit-produced media to redefine identity and create community among readers and viewers by engaging in processes of self-affirming representation denied to them as a marginalized group in the Indian context. As Mitra (2001) points out, "the re-negotiating of identity, is particularly crucial for marginalized groups," since their identity in particular cultures is always constructed as "Other" and they are defined in terms of "a specific set of identity narratives" that tend to disenfranchise their stories (p. 30). In this context, a Dalit editor explained:

> One of the things that we are trying to do by establishing these media outlets is to create a sense of our own selfhood...we want our people to experience pride in our accomplishments and to develop our own sense of history...this is really important because typically we are either invisible or we are victims in reporting. We never really see ourselves and so we try to carry content that challenges the incomplete way in which we are portrayed.

As part of the focus on strengthening a sense of collective Dalit identity outside the framework of the caste system, identified as crucial to emancipatory politics by Ambedkar, numerous Dalit-produced news sites highlight individuals who have played a significant role in Dalit history and culture. In fact, in addition to news, many of these websites have explicit sections variously tagged "Culture" as on the *Dalit Desk* homepage or "Arts, History and Culture" on the *Justice News* site. Likewise, *The Shudra* has a section titled "Bahujan Icons" (a term meaning "the majority" to underline the fact that most Indians do not belong to the upper castes) while the *Forward Press* site has a section called "Our Heroes"—to name but a few. These pages underscore the achievements of Dalit leaders, including historical figures such as Jyotiba Phule and Dr. B.R. Ambedkar as well as social reformer Kanshi Ram who is credited with founding the first national level political party representing Dalits. Additionally, these sites also profile the small number of prominent Dalits in the upper echelons of government.

Other exemplars of positive coverage include stories about Dalit scholars, interviews with Dalit artists and sports figures or even stories hailing lesser known inspirational figures. One such individual is the late Dashrath Manjhi, a villager from the state of Bihar who spent 20 years to establish a path connecting his remote, mountainous village to the outside world and was featured on multiple news sites as a symbol of Dalit effort and persistence (Dalit Desk, 2022). Many Dalit-produced news media also seek to memorialize important events in Dalit history such as the Mahad Satyagraha of 1927, when Dalits broke with social mores to drink water from a public tank that they had been forbidden to use or the anti-colonial Hul rebellion by Santhal tribes in Bengal who, as one article put it "started India's freedom movement but have not been accorded the respect that they deserve" (Chauhan, personal communication, 2022). Such coverage arguably represents an effort by Dalit journalists "to redress what they consider an imbalance of media power in mainstream media that results in the marginalization of certain social groups" (Atton, 2010, p. 170). Justifying the presence of such coverage, a Dalit reporter said that such positive stories which challenged dominant patterns of representation were necessary because "they helped people in our community to develop a positive sense of who they are or can be rather than always being defined in terms of what we lack."

While the parallel discursive arena represented by Dalit news sites thus offers their communities discursive material to engage in processes of representation and identity creation usually denied to them in the dominant public sphere, it also fosters the creation of a sense of connection or belonging between them. Indeed, just as newspapers played a central role in the creation of "imagined communities," whereby people could perceive themselves to be part of larger national collectivities (Anderson, 1983), Dalit-produced digital media play a similar role. This is particularly true of Hindi language news sites that engender patterns of mutual recognition among community members who might otherwise be separated by spatial or socio-economic location, enabling them to see themselves as part of a larger societal grouping, giving rise to communities of interest or so-called "webs of affinity" that can serve as the basis for mobilization and collective action (Nayar, 2014).

In addition to fostering a sense of identity and community, online Dalit media also seek to employ varied discursive practices to engage in "emancipationist self-representation" (Hartley, 2009, p. 310) by questioning mainstream media narratives. A notable strategy in this regard involves highlighting stories involving their community that are absent from the mainstream media. In fact, a point repeatedly made by numerous Dalit journalists was that stories involving Dalits do not get adequate attention in the mainstream media even "in the so-called progressive and independent outlets which are also casteist in their coverage," as one journalist asserted. Another Dalit reporter who had worked at various Hindi-language newspapers before launching his own outlet emphasized that mainstream media fundamentally tended to see Dalit-related issues as having limited significance and that editors routinely rejected attempts to cover them. As he put it, "they see them as small and too common to consider them news." Underscoring this point, the founder of a news portal stated:

> Due to the casteist nature of dominant media, our stories don't get any attention most of the time. They only cover us when something really bad happens, if there is a horrific gangrape or major massacre we make it to the headlines…we have to die to get covered.

Meanwhile, a woman reporter who had previously worked in mainstream news outlets before starting her own news portal and YouTube channel argued that given this situation, it was journalists from the Dalit community who had to take the lead in covering the latter. In her words:

> I always keep saying if my hand is cut only I am the one who would sense the actual pain because eventually, I am the sole sufferer of that pain. And I will be able to tell my pain better because that part belongs to me. Similarly, only people belonging to that marginalized community, will be better able to reflect on their own pain. If you see till now someone else is writing their history and those people describe that history by limiting it in a specific manner.
>
> (Singh, 2023)

Indeed, these reporters' stance seems to reflect Phillips (1996) position on political representation where she argues that "anyone cannot stand in for anyone" (p. 146), that is to say people need to speak for themselves.

A natural outgrowth of this perspective is a focus on reporting stories that pertain to their community as well as producing "re-descriptions of life-worlds" that facilitate "morally and politically enabling knowledge about Dalits," (Pandian, 2008) which can, in turn, enable them to "[challenge] the power embedded in the institutions of society for the purpose of reclaiming representation for their own values and interests" (Castells, 2015, p. 5). Not surprisingly, central to these efforts is an emphasis on stories focusing on the quotidian experiences of Dalit communities specifically as they pertain to issues of caste. In this context, Dalit news organizations prominently feature stories and videos of caste-motivated discrimination and violence against members of Dalit communities that legitimize the experiences of the latter, allowing individuals to both share and bear witness to traumatic events. Such accounts range from cases of upper caste farmers brutally attacking Dalits, including children, for daring to enter their fields and the failure of government institutions such as schools and hospitals to provide services to Dalits to sexual assaults of Dalit women and children as well as murders of Dalit youths by members of upper caste communities.

Explaining the focus on such coverage, especially in the context of rural areas, a Dalit reporter said that while upper caste reporters particularly those from rural backgrounds—in what would almost seem to be an Indian variation of Gans' small town pastoralism—tend to idealize rural life in India—members of his community experience it in markedly different ways with exclusion and assaults constituting a constant and ongoing feature of everyday life. Explaining this disjuncture, a Dalit reporter said:

> When upper caste reporters think of rural areas, they recall good times... playing in the village with friends, watching their grandmother milk a cow, seeing the crops sway in the wind. We, on the other hand, recall not being paid fairly for work or being assaulted and beaten, sometimes for a minor issue or no issue at all.

Such perceptions are also borne out by government data. According to the National Crime Records Bureau, *nearly 139,045 cases* of crimes against Dalits were registered in different states (predominantly in villages) between 2018 and 2020 and this number further increased in 2021 with women and children being increasingly targeted (Economic Times Bureau, 2021).

The sustained reportage of such occurrences, which is a defining characteristic of Dalit-focused news outlets, represents a sharp and deliberate counter to the standards of newsworthiness employed by mainstream news organizations, which tend to either underplay the continuing significance of caste in the Indian context or treat instances of caste-related oppression as remnants of a reactionary, primordial past, rather than a ubiquitous and widely institutionalized contemporary practice (Kureel, 2021). By continuously highlighting and documenting situations involving caste-related oppression that are generally erased or only marginally reported in mainstream media discourse, Dalit-produced digital media thus not only engage in "chronicling and archiving" (*Bødker & Brügger, 2018) an* alternative history but also simultaneously seek to discursively circumvent the existing regime of media (non) representation of the "lived social experiences" of Dalits.

As part of this effort to communicate counter narratives that contest those circulating in the dominant public sphere, Dalit-produced media also seek to challenge mainstream news framings of stories involving Dalit communities. As Gitlin (1980) suggests, framing involves "persistent patterns of cognition, interpretation, and presentation, of selection, emphasis, and exclusion, by which symbol-handlers routinely organize discourse..." (p. 7). In other words, frames both reflect and constitute ideological structures in society. And in the case of coverage related to Dalits—arguably underpinned by a combination of the project of Indian modernity that has long sought to "suppress" markers such as caste in the public sphere, the BJP government's more recent efforts to redefine identity in terms of faith (Chadha, 2018) as well as the absence of Dalit representatives in the news media—mainstream story framings tend to elide issues of caste. In response, Dalit media online engage in an active reframing of such news narratives, examining them specifically through the perspective of caste. Commenting on this a Dalit reporter said that when mainstream media cover instances of violence or oppression faced by marginalized communities:

> They write very cleverly to take a different angle and choose to unsee or ignore the role of caste and instead emphasize other factors…many times they avoid using the full name of perpetrators which reveal their caste identity or they tend to add a last name like Kumar from which it is impossible to tell anything about the group to which a person belongs. But when we cover the same incidents we identify these people by caste and try to connect their actions to the broader context of caste-based discrimination and attacks faced by our people on a daily basis.

In this regard, another journalist said that in the gruesome and notorious Hathras gang rape case, while mainstream coverage implied that the family of the victims were Naxalites (a term widely used in Indian political discourse to deride those who oppose the ruling BJP) and sought, in the view of Dalit outlets, to "delink the rape from its casteist origins," the latter took a very different approach by emphasizing the fact that the victim, a Dalit girl, was assaulted by four upper caste men. Put differently, they sought to emphasize that the case was not simply a crime but a caste-based crime. In a similar vein, several journalists also brought up the case of Inder Meghwal—a young Dalit student in Jalore district in the western Indian state of Rajasthan—who was allegedly beaten severely by a teacher for touching a pot of water meant for upper castes at his school and eventually died due to his injuries. As in the Hathras rape case, they said that whereas mainstream reports denied the existence of a caste angle and in fact suggested that there was no water pot, Dalit-produced media underscored the effects of caste dynamics in the area where the incident occurred. As one journalist bluntly asserted:

> Basically, in case after case mainstream media try not to bring up caste while we try to counter and offer alternative perspectives to such reporting in order to support our community.

As part of this general effort to challenge mainstream media, Dalit news outlets also report on other issues employing a specific Dalit-centric advocacy-oriented perspective. One example of this is the analysis of the annual national budget released by the Indian government that is undertaken by many Dalit news outlets principally in terms of its implications for members of their community. For instance, *The Shudra*'s 2023 budget coverage explored the cuts in the section of the budget aimed at Scheduled Castes and Tribes and questioned the diversion of funds to other sectors as unfair while the *National Dastak* organized a debate that focused exclusively on the impact of the budget on marginalized groups, with participants putting forward the Dalit point of view. Similar advocacy-oriented reporting is also manifest in relation to coverage of other types of political and cultural news as well. In fact, Dalit journalists interviewed for this project almost universally defined their journalism as aimed at supporting and advancing their community. That is to say, advocating for it. Underscoring this point, one Dalit editor said:

> Our primary goal is to empower our community. I always ask myself how can I educate my people, how can I raise awareness about their issues. I try to create a space for our perspective which does not exist in the mainstream media.

While another said that his outlet and others like it were motivated by:

> A desire to tell our own stories in a personal way, based on our experiences especially about caste because people who have not experienced caste-based discrimination or oppression cannot really write about it. When we cover things happening in our community, injustices faced by our people we have an emotional connection compared to journalists who work in the mainstream media. When Dalit men were beaten and paraded naked in Una in 2016 on suspicion that they had killed a cow, it was very personal to me because I come from a Dalit community whose members work with dead animals to make leather products. My grandfather did this kind of work…so it was not just a story for me…

Dalit-Produced Digital Media and Journalistic Values

With regard to the question of journalistic values, the majority of Dalit journalists interviewed, made the point that it is professionally trained reporters who produce the most credible reporting on Dalit issues. In other words, they expressed considerable support for values such as an adherence to truth, verification and facticity that are normatively associated with professional journalism, although many argued that they saw themselves as engaging in a superior form of "truth telling" journalism that serves the public by holding institutional structures to account in ways that mainstream media does not. However, in contrast to mainstream journalists who predicate their legitimacy claims on the basis of a presumed adherence to canonical professional values such as "neutrality" and "objectivity," Dalit reporters and editors questioned the very existence of such values, asserting that all reporting in the Indian context is influenced by the perspectives of the individual journalists as well as the structures of privilege within which they typically operate. Emphasizing this widely-held position, a journalist commented:

> We are often told that what we do is activism and not journalism. But what about mainstream outlets? They claim certain virtues but are they really objective? I don't think so. Just take a look at television channels. When

Corona was happening and there were so many problems with the government's response, did they criticize it? No, they just blamed Muslims for spreading it due to the event at the Tablighi Jamaat in Delhi. And when the BJP decided to build the Ram Mandir in Ayodhya, they were all supporting it. They just support the government. How is this being objective?

Another comparing Dalit-produced media with the Black press that played a similar role in the United States declared:

> Neutrality and objectivity are vague terms. Media in India have never been objective. Mainstream media always has a point of view which is casteist. And even so-called ally media can be discriminatory and have a caste bias. Our position is that media should support victims and if that means that people call us activists, we don't care!

Dalit media producers thus identified advocacy as crucial to their efforts to create counter discourses. This results in media sites that are "filled with struggle, protest, fantasy and opposition against bourgeois public spheres of production and communication" (Negt & Kluge, 1972). However, even as Dalit news outlets underscored articulating their community's perspectives as fundamental to their mission—a point reiterated by multiple journalists— many also saw themselves as engaging with broader society through their effect on mainstream media. In other words, they suggested that they do not see themselves simply as an "enclave" to use Squires' (2002) term but also seek to influence those in the mainstream.

In this regard, the founder of a popular news portal said that while traditional media coverage of marginalized communities such as Dalits tended to portray Dalits almost exclusively as victims,[8] the rise of Dalit-produced media and its reportage does occasionally compel legacy media to pay attention to cases of violence and discrimination against Dalits. Elaborating on this point he said, "we have an unacknowledged relationship with mainstream papers and channels…they don't openly admit it but they do look at our reporting and pick up some stories that we cover such as the Hathras incident or when our leaders' tweet about something that may have happened." Similarly, another said:

> We act as an online pressure group and force things into mainstream media discourse, things that they would not otherwise cover…and by doing that I think we actually interact with and affect broader society…when our stories get covered, people talk about them and the government takes note this strengthens democracy.

Such developments, according to Dalit journalists, although by no means typical, affected mainstream public discourse and indicated a degree of engagement and impact that did not exist prior to the emergence of digital media.

Dalit Digital Media Production: Challenges and Future

By thus facilitating the development of a sense of community identity as well as contesting and offering counter discourses to pervasive societal narratives, Dalit-produced digital media engage in actions that contribute to what Mowbray (2019) has termed counter public formation and facilitation, arguably a key activity of alternative media. At the same time however, Dalit journalists repeatedly emphasized the existence of financial limitations that materially affected their journalistic practice. In this regard, they emphasized that in addition to the majority of their audience members being unable to afford subscriptions, the latter's socio-economic status made it difficult to attract advertisers. For instance, Ashok Das, founder of *Dalit Dastak*—one of the earliest online Dalit media outlets with close to a million readers—stated that mainstream companies did not want to advertise in a "Dalit" outlet. As a result, the only advertising received by his website came from members of the Dalit community "who sometimes buy ads on the occasion of Dr. Ambedkar's birthday or some important event in our history…and on rare occasions, from government agencies "when a Dalit official puts some advertising our way."

Meanwhile, Sahil Valmiki who runs the *Dalit Desk* website, which relies almost exclusively on crowd funding, said that Dalit-produced media were often hampered by the fact that they lacked the social capital that would give them access to foundations and other entities that support alternative journalism outlets. In a similar vein, Sumit Chauhan who established *The Shudra* (and the YouTube channel *The Newsbeak*) said that although his organization and others like it received some revenues from YouTube because their content often contained footage of violence against Dalits and was flagged by YouTube as unsuitable for ad placement, this source of income was unreliable. He also underlined the fact that Dalit-produced news media were unable to attract sponsorships and external funding, recounting an interaction where a foundation expressed interest in his outlet's work but eventually did not fund it on the grounds that "they did activism and not journalism."

Such resource limitations, according to several Dalit journalists, made it difficult to not only expand and cover a large number of stories and beats but also hire trained staff who were capable of engaging in accurate and ethical reporting aimed at serving the public. Many journalists also stated that they struggled to find resources to undertake fact checking and verification especially of the videos and other social media content that they routinely receive from audience members many of whom undertake forms of sousveillance and engage in witnessing of everyday instances of caste-based discrimination and violence.

But even as Dalit-produced digital news media confront challenges, they simultaneously not only enable the dissemination of significant news and information but also engender oppositional discourses that challenge mainstream media narratives. In so doing, they have emerged as a significant form of alternative journalism, defined by many of the characteristics that Hackett and Carroll (2006) assign to such media namely, that they are "explicitly opposed to particular axes of domination," adopt a "stance of advocacy rather than pseudo-objectivity," and feature "voices and issues marginalized in hegemonic media" (p. 58).

And although the ability of such outlets to engender significant change in the contemporary formations of social and political power in India remains an evolving question (Mandal, 2020), given the economic standing of rural Dalit communities (which obviously affects their ability to support such publications) and the absence of adequate advertising support from mainstream businesses, there are a few hopeful signs. Significant among these is the fact that India is characterized by the growing penetration of smartphones, especially in rural areas where Dalit communities are predominantly located. According to the most recent Annual Survey for Education Report (ASER) while approximately 36% of rural households had a smartphone in 2018, by 2022, this has more than doubled to 74.8%. In other words, audiences interested in and able to access Dalit-oriented digital media are arguably growing rapidly outside urban areas. As a Dalit reporter who previously worked in mainstream journalism explained:

> People want to find news outlets that speak to them, for them and about them. For Dalits who are not visible or recognized in mainstream media, this means actively seeking out Dalit media, including in rural areas where the combination of word of mouth and access to cheap data leads people to such outlets.

Such developments potentially have powerful implications for Dalit news media, notably in terms of their ability to challenge the caste-based social and economic status quo that has historically characterized Indian society and media. Indeed, as Phillips (1996) argues it is only through the "politics of presence," whereby marginalized groups actually speak for themselves, that their experiences can be adequately or equitably included within political systems. This argument is equally applicable to the media. In order to ensure meaningful representation, those outside the mainstream have to take ownership of their perspectives and create their own narratives. And despite the existence of significant economic and societal constraints, such representation is what Dalit-run digital news outlets seek to provide to their communities.

Notes

1 According to Brahmanical texts such as the Manusmriti (compiled between 2 BC and 3 CE), Dalits were considered "avarna" or outside of the four "varnas" or castes that make up Hindu society. Dalit social activist Jyotiba Phule is credited with first using the term in relation to oppression faced by his community in the late 19th

century. Subsequently, the term was used by Dalit leader B.R. Ambedkar to refer to people at the bottom of the social hierarchy. By the 1970s, with the rise of the Dalit Panther movement, the term was used as a form of self-assertion and acquired a political meaning (Gulati, 2018).

2 The official term for such individuals is Scheduled Castes and Scheduled Tribes.

3 The new categories were a reclassification of so-called groups categorized as so-called depressed classes by the British.

4 B.N. Uniyal said that he undertook the exercise in response to a question from Kenneth Cooper, an African American journalist for the Washington Post who was interested in obtaining a quote from a Dalit journalist when he realized that he could not identify a single Dalit reporter.

5 Sixty six percent of Dalits can be categorized as what scholars call "multi-dimensionally" poor compared to 33% of the rest of India's population (Alkire & Santos, 2010).

6 The 2018 protests indicate another catalyzing event. These protests were held surrounding the Indian Supreme Court's efforts to amend the 1989 Scheduled Castes and Scheduled Tribes (Prevention of Atrocities) Act so that those accused of committing caste-based atrocities could obtain anticipatory bail which was disallowed under the original statute.

7 Manu's text known as the Manusmriti is believed to have been written sometime between the 2nd century BCE to 3rd century CE.

8 S. Anand has called such coverage "Visible Dalit, Invisible Brahmin" where coverage focuses on Dalits purely as objects of oppression.

References

Achanta, P. (2015, August 24). Why do these ghastly stories rarely make news headlines? *India Together*. https://indiatogether.org/crime-against-dalits-not-reported-in-media-media

Agarwal, S. (2022, October 4). In their own words Dalit writers challenge media bias. *Fair Planet*. https://www.fairplanet.org/story/in-their-own-words-dalit-journalists-challenge-media-bias/

Ahuja, A. (2018, April 23). Digital Dalits: Is social media a game changer for Dalit politics? *The Print*. https://theprint.in/opinion/dalit-history-month/digital-dalits-is-social-media-a-game-changer-for-dalit-politics/51284/

Alkire, S., & Santos, E. M. (2010). Acute multidimensional poverty: A new index for developing countries. https://papers.ssrn.com/sol3/papers.cfm?abstract_id=1815243

Ambedkar, B. R. (1993). *Dr. Babasaheb Ambedkar: Writings and speeches*. Government of Maharashtra.

Anderson, B. (1983). *Imagined communities. Reflections on the origin and spread of nationalism*. Verso Books.

Atton, C. (2010). Alternative journalism: Ideology and practice. In S. Allan (Ed.), *Routledge companion to news and journalism* (pp. 169–178). Routledge

Balasubramaniam, J. (2011). Dalits and a lack of diversity in the newsroom. *Economic and Political Weekly*, *46*(11), pp. 21–23.

Banik, P. (2016, March 15). The oppressed Indian: A monthly journal started by Kanshi Ram. *Sabrang India*. https://sabrangindia.in/article/oppressed-indian-monthly-journal-started-kanshi-ram

Bhatia, S., Sridhar, S. S., Chandna, T., & Lone, M. D. (2019). Who tells our stories matters? Representation of marginalized caste groups in Indian newsrooms. https://www.themediarumble.com/reports

Bødker, H., & Brügger, N. (2018). The shifting temporalities of online news: The Guardian's website from 1996 to 2015. *Journalism, 19*(1), 56–74.

Castells, M. (2015). *Networks of outrage and hope: Social movements in the internet age.* Polity Press.

Chadha, K. (2018). From caste to faith: Contemporary identity politics in a globalized India. *Journalism and Communication Monographs, 20* (1), 84–87.

Chandoke, N. (2005). Revisiting the crisis of representation thesis: the Indian context. *Democratization, 12*(3), 308–340.

Curran, J., & Couldry, N. (2003). *Contesting media power. Alternative media in a networked world.* Rowman & Littlefield Publishers.

Dalit Desk (2022, August 17). Dashrath Manjhi you moved the mountain but couldn't move the consciousness of caste ridden and rigid society. *Dalit Desk.* https://dalitdesk.com/dashrath-manjhi-moved-the-mountain-but-couldnt-move-the-foundation-of-caste

Dowling, D. O. (2020). Signs of a Dalit spring: India's activist magazine journalism. *Journal of Magazine Media, 21*(1), 82–106.

Economic Times Bureau (2021, December 1). Over 1.3 lakh cases of crime against Dalits since 2018; UP, Bihar, Rajasthan top charts. *Economic Times* https://economictimes.indiatimes.com/news/india/139000-cases-of-crime-against-dalits-since-2018/articleshow/88019445.cms

Fonseca, A. F., Bandhopadhya, S., Louçã, J., & Manjaly, J. A. (2019). Caste in the news: A computational analysis of Indian newspapers. *Social Media + Society, 5*(4), https://journals.sagepub.com/doi/full/10.1177/2056305119896057

Fraser, N. (1990). Rethinking the public sphere. *Social Text, 25*(26), 56–80.

Gitlin, T. (1980). *The whole world is watching. Mass media in the making and unmaking of the new left.* University of California Press.

Gulati, A. (2018, September 11). Dalit: The word, the sentiment and a 200-year old history. *The Quint.* https://www.thequint.com/news/india/dalit-history-of-term-political-social-usage#read-more

Hackett, R., & Carroll, W. (2006). *Remaking media: The struggle to democratic public communication.* Routledge.

Harad, T. (2020). *Caste is not a thing of the past: Bahujan stories from the newsroom floor.* Reuters Journalism Institute. https://reutersinstitute.politics.ox.ac.uk/sites/default/files/2020-08/RISJ_Final%20Report_Tejas%20Harad_2020_FINAL%20%282%29.pdf

Harshvardhan, & Mogha, S. (2022, July 16). Remembering Swami Achutanand: The pioneer of Dalit identity and consciousness in North India. *The Wire.* https://thewire.in/caste/remembering-swami-achutanand-the-pioneer-of-dalit-identity-and-consciousness-in-north-india

Hartley, J. (2009). Journalism and popular culture. In K. Wahl-Jorgensen, & T. Hanitzsch (Eds.), *Handbook of journalism studies* (pp. 310–324). Routledge.

Jaffrelot, C. (2016, February 18). *Dalits still left out. Indian Express.* http://indianexpress.com/article/opinion/columns/rohith-vemula-discrimination-against-dalits-still-left-out/

Jeffrey, R. (2001). [NOT] being there: Dalits and India's newspapers. *South Asia Journal of South Asian Studies, XXIV*(2), 225–238. https://doi.org/10.1080/00856400108723459

Kashyap, O. (2022). *Periyar's powerful journalism.* Forward Press. https://www.forwardpress.in/2022/01/periyars-powerful-journalism/

Kidambi, P. (2016). *The making of an Indian metropolis: Colonial governance and public culture in Bombay, 1890-1920.* Routledge.

Kerner Commission (1968). Report of the National Advisory Commission on Civil Disorders. https://www.ojp.gov/ncjrs/virtual-library/abstracts/national-advisory-commission-civil-disorders-report

Kumar, N. (2021). Social media, Dalits and the politics of presence. An analysis of the presence of Dalits in the media. *Social and Political Research Foundation*. https://sprf.in/social-media-dalits-and-politics-of-presence-an-analysis-of-the-presence-of-dalit-voices-in-the-indian-media

Kumar, C. S., & Subramani, R. (2014). Internet as an alternative media for Dalits in India: Prospects and challenges. *ISOR Journal of Humanities and Social Science, 19*(2), 125–129 https://doi.org/10.9790/0837-1925125129

Kureel, P. (2021). Indian media and caste: Of politics, portrayals and beyond. *CASTE / A Global Journal on Social Exclusion, 2*(1), 97–108.

Mandal, D. (2020, July 19). *India's oppressed had high hopes from Internet but upper castes got in there too. The Print*. https://theprint.in/opinion/indias-oppressed-groups-had-high-hopes-from-internet-but-upper-castes-got-in-there-too/463431/

Mitra, A. (2001). Marginal voices in cyberspace. *New Media & Society, 3*(1), 29–48.

Mitra, A. (2004). Voices of the marginalized on the internet: Examples from a website for South Asian women. *Journal of Communication, 54*(3), 492–510.

Mohammed, R. (2020, February 5). Why I converted to Islam and buried my Hindu identity Dalit camera founder. *The Print*. https://theprint.in/opinion/why-i-converted-to-islam-and-buried-my-hindu-identity-dalit-camera-founder/359849/

Mowbray, M. (2019). Alternative logics? Parsing the literature on alternative media. In C. Atton (Ed.), *The Routledge companion to alternative and community media* (pp. 21–31). Routledge.

Nayar, P. K. (2014). The digital Dalit: Subalternity and cyberspace. *Sri Lanka Journal of the Humanities, 37*(1–2), 69–74. https://doi.org/10.4038/sljh.v37i1-2.7204

Negt, O., & Kluge, A. (1972). *The public sphere and experience*. Verso Books.

Oza, P. (2019). Little magazines in India and the emergence of Dalit literature. GAP interdisciplinarities. *A Global Journal of Interdisciplinary Studies, 2*(3), 403–406.

Pai, S. (2020, March 25). Future of Dalit politics swings between decline and regeneration. *The Wire*. https://thewire.in/politics/dalit-politics-chandra-shekhar-aazad

Pandian, M. S. S. (2008). Writing ordinary lives. *Economic and Political Weekly, 43*(38), 34–40.

Paul, S., & Dowling, D. O. (2018). Digital archiving as social protest: *Dalit Camera* and the mobilization of India's "Untouchables. *Digital Journalism, 6*(9), 1239–1254.

Phillips, A. (1996). Dealing with difference: Politics of ideas or politics of presence? In S. Benhabib (Ed.), *Democracy and difference: Contesting the boundaries of the political* (pp. 139–152). Princeton University Press.

Pol, P. (2018, April 14). The journalistic legacy of B.R. Ambedkar. *The Wire*. https://thewire.in/caste/the-journalistic-legacy-of-b-r-ambedkar-the-editor

Poonam, S., & Bansal, S. (2023). Technology in the lives of young Dalits. In S. Pai, D. Babu, & R. Verma (Eds.), *Dalits in the new millennium* (pp. 285–301). Cambridge University Press.

Ratnamala, (2012, April 13). Ambedkar and Media. https://www.roundtableindia.co.in/ambedkar-and-media/

Rawat, R. S., & Satyanarayana, K. (2016). Introduction. In R. S. Rawat, &   K. Satyanarayana (Eds.), *Dalit studies* (pp. 1–30). Duke University Press.

Sharma, M. (2020, January 26). Celebrating Ambedkar, the journalist. *Hindustan Times* https://www.hindustantimes.com/delhi-news/celebrating-ambedkar-the-journalist/story-FJbGur4xq7E95v79jFNbBI.html

Shinde, R. (2020, October 12). From indifference to victim-blaming: Why the main-stream media's coverage of Hathras is unsurprising. *Newslaundry.* https://www.newslaundry.com/2020/10/12/from-indifference-to-victim-blaming-why-the-main-stream-medias-coverage-of-hathras-is-unsurprising

Singh, S. P. (2023, February 24). Meena Kotwal in conversation with FII. *Feminism in India.com.* https://feminisminindia.com/2023/02/24/fii-interviews-journalist-meena-kotwal/

Spivak, G. (1988). Can the subaltern speak? In C. Nelson, & L. Grossberg (Eds.), *Marxism and the interpretation of culture* (pp. 271–313). MacMillan.

Squires, C. R. (2002). Rethinking the black public sphere: An alternative vocabulary for multiple public spheres. *Communication Theory, 12*(4), 446–468.

Srivastava, D. (2022, June 15). Journalists from India's lowered castes are making their stories known. Next City. https://nextcity.org/urbanist-news/journalists-from-indias-lowered-castes-are-making-their-stories-known

Subramanyam, G. (2020, September 13). In India, Dalits still feel bottom of the caste ladder. *NBC News.* https://www.nbcnews.com/news/world/india-dalits-still-feel-bottom-caste-ladder-n1239846

Suk, J., Zhang, Y., Yue, Z., Wang, R., Dong, X., Yang, D., & Lian, R. (2023). When the personal becomes political. Unpacking the dynamics of sexual violence and gender justice discourses across four platforms. *Communication Research, 50*(5), 610–632.

Thakur, A. K. (2019). New media and the Dalit counter-public sphere. *Television and New Media, 21*(4). https://doi.org/10.1177/1527476419872133

Thapa, R., van Teijlingen, E., Regmi, P. R., & Heaslip, V. (2021). Caste exclusion and health discrimination in South Asia: A systematic review. *Asia Pacific Journal of Public Health, 33* (8). https://journals.sagepub.com/doi/full/10.1177/10105395211014648

The Wire Staff (2019, January 17). My birth is my fatal accident: Rohith Vemula's searing letter is an indictment of social prejudices. *The Wire.* https://thewire.in/caste/rohith-vemula-letter-a-powerful-indictment-of-social-prejudices

Thirumal, P., & Tartikov, G. M. (2011). India's Dalits search for a democratic opening in the digital divide. In P. R. Leigh (Ed.), *International exploration of technology equity and the digital divide: Critical, historical and social perspectives* (pp. 20–39). Information Science Reference.

Uniyal, B. N. (1996). In search of a Dalit journalist. Broadsheet on contemporary politics. *Anveshi.org.* https://www.anveshi.org.in/broadsheet-on-contemporary-politics/archives/broadsheet-on-contemporary-politics-vol-2-no-1011/in-search-of-a-dalit-journalist/

Yadav, Y. (2022, October 27). Hindu upper-caste Indian media is a lot like White-dominated South Africa. *The Print.* https://theprint.in/opinion/hindu-upper-caste-indian-media-is-a-lot-like-white-dominated-south-africa/1184213/

Yadav, Y., Chamaria, A., & Kumar, J., (2006, June 6). National media devoid of social diversity: Survey. *Maharashtra Herald*, p. 7a.

3 Muslim-Produced Online News

Reclaiming Voice?

Background

"Working in mainstream media, I realized that news related to marginalized communities like Muslims does not get covered. Outlets like ours show their concerns and perspectives. We don't claim to get them justice but we give space to their voice," said the young female founder of *Pal Pal News*, India's only YouTube news channel run exclusively by Muslim women. Meanwhile, one of the founders of *Maktoob Media*, a site which describes itself as "an independent news outlet that delivers handpicked newsworthy stories focusing on human rights, minorities and policies," said that his outlet published from "a Muslim perspective...from a community point of view...because that's what I saw was lacking, and I thought that is what I need to be doing that I need to put up the voice of the community in front of the world...tell people that this is what the community thinks about any particular issue." Similarly, an independent female Muslim reporter who previously worked for *The Cognate*—which defines itself as "a digital news platform of Indian Muslim news, ideas, culture, and business"—said "the mainstream media have completely neglected the voices of Muslims...the issues that are being faced by them, the things that they are going through...so that's what we try to highlight for them." Collectively, these journalists represent a growing trend in which young Muslim journalists have established digital news outlets that strive to "narrate stories of the community and other marginalized groups from a perspective different from the majoritarian viewpoint" (Agha, 2022).

The presence of media outlets aimed at Indian Muslims is not an entirely novel development in India where several Urdu newspapers aimed at the community have long been a part of the print media terrain. However, the majority of these print publications are produced by mainstream media corporations, which also publish Hindi papers[1] and routinely tend to reproduce generic content across their outlets. As one Muslim journalist put it, "much of the news is very general and a lot of it is just stuff from their other papers just translated into Urdu, there is very little that is actually tailored to the community or reflects their perspectives." There are also a handful of community-based publications such as the *Radiance Weekly*. Publishing since the 1960s, the

DOI: 10.4324/9781003244202-3

magazine which is ideologically aligned with the views of the *Jamaat-e-Islami*, a Muslim religious-political organization, has "never had the freedom that is requisite for effective journalism, nor has it attracted high caliber journalists," according to a Muslim journalist.

In contrast, the new outlets which are digital entirely in nature, typically take the form of news-oriented websites, YouTube channels or Facebook pages. Commenting on their emergence, the founder of *TwoCircles.net*, the earliest Muslim-produced and oriented news site said:

> The Muslim community has always felt that we need to have news outlets but it is digital technologies that have made it possible, they been really empowering…it has allowed a kind of leapfrogging so that these outlets can be read by people in Kerala or Kashmir.

Some of these outlets, while editorially autonomous (Iyer, 2022), openly indicate their affiliation with the Muslim community adopting names such as *Maktoob Media*, *Milli Gazette*, *Millat Times* and *Muslim Mirror*, whereas others like *Hindustan Gazette*, *TwoCircles.net*, *Clarion India* and *The Cognate* (see Figures 3.1 and 3.2) as well as nationally-oriented YouTube channels

Figure 3.1 Screenshot from *Maktoob Media*, a Muslim produced news site.

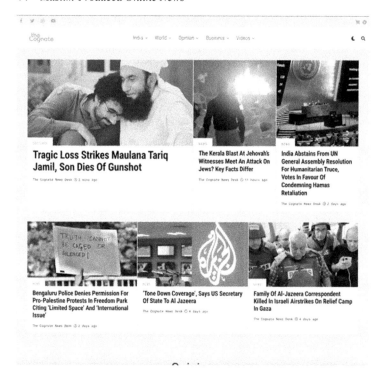

Figure 3.2 Screenshot from *The Cognate*, a Bangalore-based Muslim produced news site.

such as *Pal Pal News* tend to avoid using the term Muslim—instead defining themselves as independent—in tag lines or thumbnails to avoid instant stigmatization. Linguistically, many of these digital outlets (especially YouTube channels) tend to operate using a mixture of colloquial Urdu and Hindi while some websites offer news in local Indian languages such as Bengali, Hindi and Malayalam.[2] However, the most novel development in the Muslim-produced digital news arena is the emergence of several English language sites (Agha, 2022; Iyer, 2022), a point emphasized by multiple journalists. Explaining this development, a journalist said that the rise of English language digital outlets is driven by "the rise of a new kind of Muslim, who is educated, speaks English and is up with technology…," while the founder of an English language news site bluntly asserted "I'm not comfortable with any other language. I don't know how to speak or read any other language I went to an English school. I actually speak to well, all my friends. Muslim or all Muslim in English…."

In terms of content, these digital outlets vary in their focus and consequently the types of stories they cover. Thus, whereas some tend to have a broader news agenda, combining general interest national news stories with international items (such as coverage of the Palestine-Israel conflict) that they perceive to be of interest to members of the Muslim community, others center their reporting on documenting lynchings and hate crimes impacting Muslims and other marginalized communities, while yet others (mainly YouTube channels and Facebook pages) approach news from a regional/local perspective. However, such variations notwithstanding, broadly speaking, these news entities position themselves as enabling Muslims to represent themselves as well as offering alternatives to the dominant trend in mainstream Indian media as it relates to Muslims, namely the lack of meaningful representation as well as the demonization of the community (Iyer, 2022).

Muslims in Indian Society and Media: Background and Contemporary Developments

Historically, the presence of Muslims in India can be traced to medieval times that witnessed a series of invasions, which started in the 10th century when so-called Turkic tribes entered India from the northwest.[3] By the 13th century, Muslim warlords established the Delhi Sultanate and controlled significant parts of northern India and gradually expanded their dominion over other parts of the sub-continent. Muslim rule culminated in the rise of the Mughal empire in the mid-16th century, which gradually lost power to the East India Company in the mid-18th century and was ultimately completely replaced by the British colonial government (Robb, 2002). As a group, Muslims have historically occupied a complex space in India's sociopolitical landscape. On the one hand, as Kaviraj (1995) points out, contemporary Indian society accommodated "the two types of Islamic groups—military entrants and the large masses of indigenous converts," (p. 170) who had arguably converted to Islam to improve their social standing in a social order where caste determined virtually every aspect of quotidian life," while "on the other, this accommodation was limited to transactional economic and business relationships. Put differently, Hindus and Muslim communities lived as Kaviraj puts it "back to back," with little contact except in certain limited arenas (p. 171).

This situation, according to him, was fundamentally changed by the arrival of British colonial rule which through its emphasis on enumeration of particular groups through census and mapping activities "fundamentally altered the logic of community identities," marking the world of those affected "indelibly by these fatal lines of distinction," as well as by "the demands of the modern politics of numbers" (Kaviraj, 1995, p. 172). Indeed, he suggests that colonial policies such as separate electorates "contributed to a constant exacerbation of frictions between religious communities" that "created the conditions for the emergence of communal politics in the last phase of colonial rule." The term communal generally refers to inter-religious conflicts in the Indian context. This arguably contributed to the partition of India in 1947, as many members of the Muslim minority felt that they could "secure themselves only in a state of their own" (Kaviraj, 1995, p. 173).

And though in the years following independence from the British in 1947, the newly-established Indian state sought to present the country as a secular, multi-religious society characterized by "an ability to transform invasion into accommodation, rupture into continuity, division into diversity," (Khilnani, 1997, p. xvi), in reality, "the nature of India's self-hood" was far more contested than the ritually celebratory accounts of Indian nation-building would suggest" (Chadha & Kavoori, 2008, p. 131). That is to say, even as official discourse articulated the notion of "unity in diversity," in reality, Indian society was characterized by multiple divisions. As Khilnani (1997) writes:

> The truncated colonial territories inherited by the Indian state after 1947 left it in control of a population of incomparable differences: a multitude of Hindu castes and outcastes, Muslims, Sikhs, Christians, Buddhists, Jains and tribes; speakers of more than a dozen major languages (and thousands of dialects); myriad ethnic and cultural communities. This discordant material was not the stuff of which nation states are made. (p. 151)

Indeed, contestation over identity has remained a defining feature of India's postcolonial polity. And even as the Indian state sought to address traditional divisions in the period following independence by promoting a pan-Indian national identity, such efforts were not especially successful in mitigating long-standing identity-based differences in the country, notably those between Hindus and Muslims. In fact, Muslims in post-colonial India were frequently stigmatized as "outsiders" or "invaders" primarily on the basis of their religious identity, even though most Indian Muslims are descendants of lower-caste Hindus who arguably converted to Islam to better their social status (Jaffrelot, 1996). As Khan (2020) points out, not only were Muslims viewed by many Hindus as responsible for the partition of India but were also seen as an "unreliable fifth column who threatened the unity and strength of the Hindu nation" (p. 57).

Such sentiments gathered further momentum with the resurgence of the Hindutva ideology in the late 1980s and early 1990s. Initially emerging in the 1920s, the term Hindutva (which means Hindu-ness) was coined by the Hindu nationalist V.D. Savarkar who called for the definition of India as a Hindu nation. Politically, this belief has become the defining ideology of the *Bharatiya Janata Party*, which has governed India for the past decade. Indeed, the party—in a curious reprise of colonial historical patterns where the British governmentality relied on classifying and actively dividing Indians along ethnic and religious lines—has sought to fundamentally redefine "Indian" identity in terms of the country's majority Hindu faith (Chadha, 2018). Not surprisingly, the foundation of this project has been the "notion of an essentialist difference with a Muslim other" (Nizaruddin, 2021, p. 1103).

As part of their adherence to Hindutva, the *Bharatiya Janata Party* (BJP) and its various affinity organizations such as the *Rashtriya Swayamsevak Sangh* (RSS) have called for "awakening" Hindus to what they perceive to be the "forced negation of Hindu history and factors that gave pride to Hindus" (BJP.org quoted in Chadha, 2018). The party has moreover argued that the "secular" Congress government, which had governed the country almost continuously since independence, had "appeased" and "pampered" minorities (code for Muslims) and presented themselves as offering "a government that would not take Hindu sentiments for granted" (Chadha, 2018). In other words, it has called into question the notion of the India as an imagined community based on a shared secular national identity, replacing it with the notion of a Hindu "rashtra" or nation—a key characteristic of the Hindutva mind set.

With the electoral victory of the BJP at the national level in 2014, and then again in 2019, the sectarian approach to politics that defines the Hindutva project has been further amplified through the promotion of an explicitly Hindu nationalist agenda. While this has been manifested tangibly in vigilante violence aimed at Muslims typically on the grounds of cow slaughter, typically with the tacit support of the BJP government (Human Rights Watch, 2019), arguably, even more pervasive is the symbolic violence directed against Muslims by the ruling party and its various Hindu affinity organizations. One form of such symbolic violence is the persistent vilification of Muslims. This is manifest in efforts to identify Muslims as descendants of medieval invaders, condemn them as "outsiders" and call into question their patriotism while also defining them as representing a clear and present threat to Hindu communities by "overbreeding" and "luring Hindu women through love jihad"[4] to convert them to Islam (Khan, 2020). Muslims also face attacks via ongoing initiatives to change textbooks to downplay the achievements of Muslim rulers (Raj, 2023), efforts to polarize the electorate in key states along religious lines as well as calls for an economic boycott of Muslim businesses by BJP politicians (Sikdar, 2023)—all undertaken presumably to exclude the community economically, politically and culturally.

Interestingly, an integral component of such government-sponsored efforts aimed at marginalizing India's largest minority community is mainstream news media who "re-present" reality (Hall, 1997) as it relates to Muslims along two primary axes. The first of these—in line with commercial media coverage of other marginalized groups—is to largely ignore the Muslim community and the issues that it faces as "one of the most socio-politically and economically deprived communities in the country" (Chatterjee, 2017, p. 1). Elaborating on this tendency, the founder of *Milli Gazette* said:

> Our print and electronic media does not have a Muslim beat. Even Israelis have Jewish journalists living in Palestinian Arab areas to directly report on issues affecting the people in these areas. This is not the case here...

The other axis is the pervasive "othering" and often outright demonization of Muslims, manifest in coverage produced by Hindi language newspapers as well as right-leaning television channels in different languages, including

English. For example, a study which examined the image of Muslims in four leading English language newspapers between 2007 and 2017 found that not only was Muslim-centered coverage minimal, but that when reporting was undertaken, it tended to be more negative than positive with members of the community being frequently deemed "terrorists, anti-nationals, communal, fundamentalists, fanatics…" (Liyakat, 2017; Sikander, 2021). Meanwhile, an analysis of two leading prime-time English talk shows—which play a crucial agenda setting role in the Indian context—showed that the headlines related to Muslims routinely used adversarial, negative language describing Muslim men as "jihadis" and "ISIS recruiters" and including words like "EXPOSE," "CAUGHT" in relation to events related to the community, thereby priming audiences to "think of Muslims as criminals," who plot against innocent Hindus (Drabu, 2018).

As such, the general "content, tone, and tenor" of these shows reinforced essentialist stereotypes by emphasizing the "oppression of Muslim women by Muslim men," while also linking Islam with "backwardness, ignorance, and violence" (Drabu, 2018). Prompted by such coverage which tends to prime audiences to view Muslims unfavorably, the chairman of the Press Council of India—a statutory regulatory agency—publicly accused the Indian media of "deliberately" dividing people on religious lines and called out its tendency to disparage "all Muslims in the country as terrorists and bomb throwers" in 2011 (Raghuram, 2011), albeit to little effect.

Such negative patterns of representation were amply manifest during the COVID-19 pandemic, when Muslims who had gathered for a religious meeting in India's capital New Delhi and were later found to be COVID positive, were deemed to be "super spreaders," who were engaged in a Corona Jihad against the nation (Sikander, 2021). In fact, the notion that as a community, Muslims are engaged in a concerted effort to conduct Jihad or holy war against Hindus is a pervasive trope in mainstream media narratives. This trope is evoked in a variety of contexts such as interreligious relationships (love jihad), conflicts over land (land jihad) as well as those over population, by both television channels and newspapers, the majority of which are openly and stridently aligned with the ruling BJP (Jain, 2023; Raj & Jafri, 2023).

At the same time, Muslim journalists in mainstream newsrooms, who comprise about 3% of the national media despite being over 14% of the population (Mujtaba, 2022), find themselves increasingly beleaguered. Although discrimination and lack of representation of Muslim journalists is a longstanding problem—with newspapers only employing "one token Muslim journalist" to cover "Eid, mushairas (poetry recitations) and madrassas," as a reporter put it—this situation has worsened markedly since the BJP's rise to power. Lamenting this circumstance, a reporter said that while previously he had felt comfortable in his newsroom, in recent years, anti-Muslim "bigotry" in newsrooms had become more pronounced, "manifesting in comments, masquerading as jokes, and dictating editorial decisions including the framing of headlines as well as the selection and display of the stories" (Ghosh, 2022). Expressing his dismay, another Muslim journalist said that while:

> A story about Hindus and Muslims uniting for a cause is played down, but news about a Hindu-Muslim rift is highlighted. If a Muslim does something good, the news will be relegated to page 7 or 8. If a Muslim does something bad, the report will be flashed on page one.
>
> (Ghosh, 2022)

Yet another reporter explained that when a Muslim graveyard ran out of space during the COVID-19 pandemic, he was told not to "highlight COVID-19 deaths in the community. But, when the state government started distributing free rations, he was told to write a story about how Muslims were also receiving help." Overall, Muslim journalists reported feeling alienated in newsrooms. As one editor put it:

> The overall atmosphere of the country has become polluted, and the result is that Muslim journalists are also being targeted in the newsrooms, hate speeches have become the order of the day, and in such a scenario, it is impossible for Muslim journalists not to face barbs.
>
> (Ghosh, 2022)

Additionally, according to the Committee to Protect journalists, Muslim reporters are also being targeted in a variety of online and offline attacks, typically by supporters of the ruling party (Bhat & Chadha, 2022).

Predictably, the combination of "othering" in society and the silencing of Muslim journalists in mainstream newsrooms has significant implications for the community's ability to have a voice and be heard in society. This is a key issue because as Couldry (2010) suggests, voice both as process i.e. the ability to speak and as value, i.e. to be heard, constitute fundamental rights that are critical to the ability of individuals to envision themselves as citizens. Drawing on a variety of philosophical traditions, Couldry emphasizes the importance of allowing human beings to give an account of their lives by "providing a narrative" (p. 7), and states that because "what we do already comes embedded in narratives, our own and that of others," to "deny another's capacity for narrative—to deny her potential for voice—is to deny a basic dimension of human life" (p. 7). He goes on to make the point that having a voice requires certain pre-conditions, namely "all the shared resources of material life, and the specifically social resources (including but not limited to language) that enable and sustain the practices of language" (p. 7).

That is to say, there are both "practical" and "symbolic" elements to the ability to have voice, which is moreover socially grounded and reflexive in the sense that narratives do not exist in a vacuum but involve "exchanges between ourselves and others" and "articulating the world from a distinctive embodied position" (p. 8). But even as Couldry underscores the importance of voice, he acknowledges that all individuals do not have equal access to the elements that make such self-narratives possible. And this inequity, where due to specific societal and institutional structures, "the materials from which some people must build their accounts of themselves are "*not* theirs to adapt and control," he argues, engenders "a deep denial of voice, a deep form of oppression" (p. 9). As he puts it,

> Voice is undermined when societies become organized on the basis that individual, collective and distributed voice, need not be taken into account because a higher value rationality trumps them. (p. 10)

While Couldry identifies neo-liberalism as a form of "voice-denying rationality," the same claim can arguably be made for Hindutva in the Indian context. Much like neo-liberalism, Hindutva has emerged as a pervasive force impacting politics, economy and society through the actions of an authoritarian populist state that not only has "naturalized" majoritarian sentiments but which defines itself (both discursively and materially) as standing "against a secular, "anti-national" liberal "elite" whose members are viewed as "pandering to non-Hindu minority groups," such as Muslims (Chacko, 2018). Expressed differently, BJP has adopted a form of "banal" nationalism involving the "everyday flagging," of the nation in the lives of citizens,"—albeit with only Hindus being seen as such—and Muslims being variously erased or pathologized in the public sphere. As one Muslim journalist put it:

> The Indian media, serious or godi (lapdog) is not concerned about Muslims. You can check any day and the 200 million Muslims of India are absent… they do not appear in the India media except in bad, one sided news.

Similar observations about the growing inability to gain fair or adequate representation in the news media, following the successive victories of the BJP, were also made by other Muslim reporters and editors. As one editor put it:

> It seems our community does not exist…most of the time Indian Muslim issues are either neglected or twisted to show the community in a bad light, knowing full well that this politically and economically weak community is unable to fight back or damage the interests of media houses.

Describing the manner in which Muslims are increasingly portrayed in the news media, several other Muslim journalists contended that while biased and inadequate media representation of their community had always been an issue, the problems had intensified after the present-day BJP government was elected. Indeed, they asserted that Muslims typically appeared only in stories that highlighted their so-called "backward" practices such as the right of men to divorce their wives by simply uttering talaq (the word for divorce) three times; as supporters of "fatwas" or decrees issued by Muslim religious leaders or as societal "threats" who were engaged in "anti-national activities," undermining the Hindu faith by killing cows while plotting the forcible conversion of Hindu women to Islam through so-called love jihad.

Such accounts that present themselves as "naturalized representations of events and situations" not only have what Hall (1981) calls "racist premises and propositions inscribed in them as a set of unquestioned assumptions" but also play a significant role in priming the minds of viewers with "unconscious racism towards Muslims and Islam." In fact, the founder of a news site made the point that Muslims are automatically seen as "mujrims" or criminals in a variety of news stories. Another journalist who compared the current state of Muslims to members of India's historically marginalized lowest castes said:

> The biggest issue post-Modi is the effort to demoralize the Muslim community. You cannot kill 200 million people or throw them into the sea.
> Instead they want to turn us into Shudras or untouchables by silencing us.

Journalistic Practices Aimed at Reclaiming "Voice"

In attempting to counter their lack of voice—especially as process—in Indian society, a frequent practice employed by Muslim-run digital news outlets is to challenge the prevalent stereotypical regime of news media representation that establishes a "frontier between insiders and outsiders, Us and Them," critical to the maintenance of "the social and symbolic order" that ultimately underpins political hegemony (Hall, 1997, p. 258). Crucial to such resistance are efforts to present Muslims in everyday contexts, "as normal people, who are just like everyone else," as the founder of *The Cognate* website explained, while another observed that:

> We have this idea that covering Muslim stories means covering violence, trauma, and Islamophobia, which in and of itself is not only taxing but a limited way to look at the totality of what it means to be a Muslim in India…We need more stories that center us as people…

> (Ghosh, 2022)

Emphasizing this point, several Muslim journalists said that their outlets made it a priority to write stories about Muslims in everyday contexts. This included stories about Muslim families engaged in routine activities such as eating and shopping (Bhattacharya, 2023), having friendships with Hindu neighbors (Khan, 2022), exhibiting art (*Millat Times* Staff, 2021) or putting on theater performances (Mattoo & Shabir, 2023). Further exemplifying this trend, Muslim news outlets carry articles about Muslim entrepreneurs and business people (Hussain 2022;) and NGOs while slide shows on the *TwoCircles.net* site showed Muslims observing Ramadan using non-typical images such as those of a woman preparing to pray while another read the Quran, people napping in a mosque, a young boy wearing jeans rather than traditional dress in a mosque and individuals eating during Ramadan to illustrate that not everyone fasts during the holy month. As the founder of *TwoCircles* put it:

> Even news outlets like Al-Jazeera tend to be stereotypical in their representation of the Muslim community…I would almost say there's a type of laziness at work. By doing photo essays of this type, we are trying to get away from stereotypes. You know the best thing to fight your stereotype is not to present another stereotype, right?

Along with portraying Muslims as individuals who engage in mundane, quotidian activities, these digital news outlets also seek to disrupt the mainstream Indian media framing of Muslims almost exclusively as "conservative" people "who present themselves in a traditional way—men with beards and skullcaps and women with burqas and niqabs" (Drabu, 2018), instead seeking to highlight the complex and diverse nature of the 200 million-strong Muslim community in India.

Consequently, a key and deliberate component of such online coverage is to include stories about women—who although observant Muslims—defy popular tropes about "oppressed" and "submissive" Muslim women (Navarro, 2010). For instance, *TwoCircles.net*—which pioneered the trend of digital Muslim news outlets—has routinely reported on ordinary women such as a burqa wearing autorickshaw driver in Chennai (Mujtaba, 2023), a Kashmiri Islamic scholar and activist Mubeena Ramzan who has been offering women advice on their property, educational and other rights within Islam (Shabir, 2023; Javeed, 2018) or young women who have worked to improve their communities such as 18-year old student Maryam Mirza who was instrumental in launching over 30 children's Mohalla or neighborhood libraries in her hometown (Fatima, 2023). Similarly, outlets also regularly seek to publicize the accomplishments of Muslim women such as nurses whose exemplary service was recognized by the president of India Ahmad (2022), local and regional female politicians (MG Correspondent, 2022; *Muslim Mirror* Staff, 2023), scientists (*Cognate News Desk*, 2023), bureaucrats, South Asian women elected to political office in the United States as well as the first female Muslim federal judge in the United States whose appointment was featured across multiple outlets (*Muslim Mirror* Staff, 2023; *Maktoob* Staff, 2023).

These outlets also frequently report on what journalists called the "positive" accomplishments of Muslim individuals and institutions, with some outlets such as *TwoCircles.net* and the *Muslim Mirror* institutionalizing the practice by establishing specific sections containing such stories on their respective sites.

In this regard, many outlets made it a point to carry stories acknowledging that the *Jamia Millia Islamia* University—an institution primarily serving Muslims students—had been highly ranked in the Ministry of Education's

National Institutional Rankings Framework. Other stories recognized those who had achieved high ranks in national school examinations, successfully "cracked" the prestigious Indian civil service examination and had been promoted to senior positions in the bureaucracy or received awards. And although these might appear to be the typical "feel good" stories usually associated with community-oriented news outlets, Muslim journalists repeatedly reiterated that such stories were essential for their community which perceived itself to be unseen and unheard, particularly in an affirmative sense. Furthermore, many journalists specifically referenced the importance of such affirming stories for young people, arguing that they were necessary to counteract the negative images of the community that Muslim youth typically encountered in media and popular culture. As one writer for the *Millat Times* explained:

In the current hostile environment where Muslims are constantly attacked and shown in a bad light by the news media, it is not just the majority community that is influenced. It also has a negative effect on Muslims too particularly the youth…that's why it is really important that we offer them role models that they can look up to…

Another said:

Growing up, especially in the period after 9/11, I always encountered people saying why are you guys always doing these kinds of things? Why are Muslims violent? Some of these questions were coming from my friends. This really affected me…

In addition, Muslim journalists also emphasized their efforts to highlight the contributions of community members whom they perceive to have been rendered invisible in mainstream news narratives. Exemplifying this trend are stories about Muhammad Baqir, the founder of an anti-British Urdu newspaper and the first journalist to be executed by the British, following the uprising of 1857, generally acknowledged as the starting point of the Indian national movement (Hussain & ul Haleem, 2023). It is also manifest in feature stories about the impact of scientific discoveries and inventions made by Muslims (*Cognate* News Desk, 2023) or the contributions of Muslim freedom fighters and leaders to India's freedom struggle against the British (*Clarion India*, 2021; Shireen, 2022). Such reporting, they suggested, was essential especially in the light of events such as the recent decision to remove mention of several key Muslim intellectuals and political figures from university curricula, particularly in BJP-dominated northern India. As an essay on the news site, *Maktoob Media* expressed it:

This year, Delhi University decided to remove poet-philosopher Mohammad Iqbal from its Political Science syllabus, specifically from a chapter titled "Modern Indian Political Thought" in the B.A. program's sixth semester. The university's vice-chancellor, Yogesh Singh, who chaired the meeting, defended the resolution by stating that individuals who played a key role in India's partition should not be included in the curriculum... However, it is crucial to contextualize this decision within a broader framework that encompasses numerous measures directed towards erasing and marginalizing Muslim intellectuals and the role they've played in Indian history.

(Wani, 2023)

Muslim journalists also made the case that integral to their efforts to question the existing representational paradigm is reporting on the views of individuals and issues that are deemed to fall into what Hallin (1986) termed the sphere of deviance. An exemplar of this type of coverage includes numerous stories across these digital news outlets related to Sharjeel Imam, a student activist who has been imprisoned since 2020 and charged under various statutes for his involvement in protests against the BJP-sponsored Citizenship Amendment Act. This piece of legislation proposed to fast-track Indian citizenship for non-Muslim migrants from Afghanistan, Bangladesh and Pakistan, and has been perceived by many as potentially leading to the disenfranchisement of Indian Muslims (Akins, 2020).

Also included in this category is reportage about the Muslim-majority state of Kashmir—whose previously autonomous constitutional status was abolished by the BJP government in 2019—which has since witnessed considerable political unrest. Unlike mainstream news organizations that tend to support the policies of the central government vis-a-vis Kashmir (Nadaf, 2021), Muslim-produced digital news sites instead regularly cover the detentions and disappearances of Kashmiri youth at the hands of security forces as well as the suppression of local journalists in the region. They also seek to humanize Kashmiris as they struggle to conduct everyday life and work, while navigating curfews and frequent government-sponsored internet shutdowns. As a whole, such oppositional reporting practices allow the Muslim community not only to contest "fixed," dominant representations produced by mainstream media narratives Hall (1997) but also to produce a narrative of self-interpretation crucial to meaningful human existence (Ricoeur, 1984). Commenting on this a journalist said, "we are simply trying to reveal the reality of our broader community...to give voice to ourselves at a time when we are unheard...considered second-class citizens in India." In other words, the activities of Muslim-produced news media thus illustrate how in Couldry's terms, voice is a "socially grounded" process, with reporting being driven by an ambient but constant awareness of the community's lack of voice.

In conjunction combatting mainstream media erasure and stereotyping, Muslim digital outlets also seek to address issues of voice by investigating and documenting what journalists typically termed "human rights abuses" and "hate crimes" against Muslims. Commenting on this approach to journalism, one of the founders of the English language news website *Maktoob* Media said:

> As a media house run by marginalized people, our niche is human rights violations and minority issues in India…70 percent of our news focuses on these themes. Why? Well when you read a news story, even if it is a story about the lynching of Muslims, they always seem to raise suspicions about the community. After reading the article, it seems that Muslims are doing something wrong and deserve to be killed for that. Anti-Muslim narratives are everywhere in the mainstream media. We don't necessarily want to spend all our time reporting on these narratives…on violence…on these daily anti-Muslim hate crimes but unfortunately this is what is happening in India.

While periodic conflicts between Hindus and Muslims or what are in local parlance referred to as "communal riots," have been a fairly regular feature of India's post-independence polity (Varshney, 2002), the successive electoral victories of the BJP have arguably given rise to a new kind of mob-based violence in which Hindu vigilantes (associated with the party or its affinity organizations) have attacked Muslims, in some cases, fatally. The majority of these attacks are linked to accusations of cow slaughter and beef eating or interfaith relationships (Mander, 2018). Although national data on lynchings are unavailable—since the National Crime Records Bureau discontinued collecting such data in 2017 claiming that "crimes" such as lynching or mob violence had not been defined under Indian law and hence data related to them were "unreliable" (Bhardwaj, 2021)—evidence collected by non-governmental agencies indicates a steep rise in hate crimes or crimes where individuals have been targeted for their identity, primarily religion. The Citizens Religious Hate Crimes Watch tracker[5] developed by non-profit data journalism initiative IndiaSpend documented 254 incidents of hate crimes motivated by religious hatred, which resulted in 91 deaths and 579 injuries between 2009 and 2018, with more than 90% of religious hate crimes—principally directed against Muslims by Hindus in BJP governed states—having occurred after the party's national victory in 2014 (Mander, 2018).

Amnesty International which also tracked hate crimes in India documented 902 hate crimes between 2015 and June 2019, with 44 people—36 of them Muslim—being killed and approximately 280 people being injured by vigilante groups affiliated with the RSS, a leading Hindutva organization (Amnesty International, 2018). These figures, according to observers, actually represent a significant undercount (Dey, 2017; Mander, 2018), with some arguing that these data were compiled exclusively from English-language papers that potentially overlooked cases. Yet others have asserted that since news media tend to only report on incidents involving deaths or significant violence, figures of cases where people were threatened, humiliated or beaten are not involved in such analyses.

With mainstream media tending to ignore or downplay anti-Muslim violence, Muslim news sites actively undertake the in-depth coverage of lynchings and other instances of physical violence experienced by Muslims. Their emphasis on such coverage is most evident in original field reporting-based stories on "hate crimes" against members of the community that are featured prominently across Muslim digital news outlets. Moreover, these sites also focus on giving those affected the opportunity to actively narrate and share their experiences with other community members. Underlining this point, one journalist said:

> The physical attacks on the Muslim community, they're happening and there's a lot of fear in the Muslim community about what's going on, about the future. People want to know what's going on. But there are also a lot of people sitting on the fringe and are not really aware of things and they're disinterested in what's happening with the community. But they are all potential consumers of the news and we want to reach them.

While highlighting attacks on members of their community, Muslim digital news outlets focus particularly on countering accounts of lynchings that appear in mainstream media. In this regard, multiple Muslim journalists asserted that whereas mainstream news outlets often sought to "frame" lynchings and assaults as unrelated to religious identity and the product of interpersonal conflicts between individuals (Chakraborty, 2017), they sought to demonstrate otherwise. They also underscored efforts to challenge the manner in which many Hindi-language newspaper stories tended to valorize vigilantes involved in the attacks while calling the victims "cow smugglers" engaged in illegal activities. Elaborating this point an editorial said:

> The role of newspapers in giving legitimacy to lynchers by calling a violent mob "rakshak" [protector] or "gau bhakt," is a common practice in Hindi papers in North India… this needs to be said clearly and more forcefully now as India has seen rise in hate crimes and mob attacks in recent years. There are circumstances that are created which embolden the members of these self-styled Senas and Dals.[6] And vernacular media plays a significant role in it.
>
> (Alavi, 2019)

Highlighting several such cases, the editorial detailed the coverage of a lynching case that occurred in 2019 in the central Indian state of Madhya Pradesh as an exemplar of such reporting. In this regard, it said, local vigilantes attacked a group of Muslim truck owners claiming that they were "cattle transporters" engaged in "trafficking" meat, the editorial pointed out that "one of the Hindi papers on the front page offered a headline that termed them as valiant warriors…while another Hindi paper highlighted the vigilantes' excesses, but still termed them 'gau-bhakts'—i.e. those who serve the cows or cow protectors" (Alavi, 2019).

Meanwhile, other observers have argued that mainstream news media coverage of lynching in India parallels the so-called "factual" coverage of lynching by 19th century American papers, which highlighted the so-called "crimes" of African Americans, community demands for immediate punishment, the inability of local authorities to provide immediate action, which in turn resulted in justified mob violence[7] (Ali, 2018). Comparing such coverage with Indian reporting on lynchings, Ali writes:

> The reports detail the accusations, pondering over the contents of the truck of the cattle trader or, as in the case of Akhlaq, the contents of his fridge… Like the 19th century Southern newspapers, our media often shy away from providing the social and political context in which the lynching took place, and focus inordinately on the 'crime' that prompted it.

In contrast, Muslim-run digital outlets—employing a combination of original reporting and citizen witnessing *by individuals*—seek to quantify and document assaults and lynchings ignored by the mainstream news media, representing the events from the perspectives of their victims. These accounts thus not only center the experiences of Muslims who have been targeted but deem them to be legitimate and authoritative sources in a manner that mainstream media, especially the Hindi and other vernacular language press, tend to deny minority victims of religiously motivated attacks in the Indian context. In doing so, they "not only blend facts with values" but also simultaneously develop "new ways of counter-surveilling and bypassing traditional gate-keepers such as professional gatekeepers" (Vasudevan (2019), pp. 3–4). That is to say, they engage in a journalism practice that "privileges" the stories of the under-represented over institutional narratives (Atton, 2010).

This effort takes diverse forms. For example, some outlets have special sections—typically identified by names such as Hate Crimes or Human Rights—containing stories that report specifically on attacks on Muslims and occasionally, other marginalized communities such as Christians and Buddhists. Others tend to have reportage spread across different areas but employ tags such as "communalism," "hate crimes" or "cow vigilantes" that enable interested readers to find stories on these topics. In fact, inputting these terms into the search functions of these outlets typically reveals multiple pages of stories highlighting the pervasiveness of the violence. Some outlets such as the *Muslim Mirror* have also developed an online Hate Crimes database whose stated goal is to "track and document all hate crimes carried out against India's 200 million Muslims, with the objective of catching all data regarding date, location, motive, victim, perpetrator and subsequent legal action."

In addition to recording the wide range of mob violence directed against Muslims which covers a spectrum ranging from forcing Muslims to chant Hindu religious slogans and removing their skull caps to attacks on mosques and violent assaults resulting in death, these digital outlets also play a crucial role in upholding and disseminating the truth claims of their community. This is especially notable in view of the pervasive reluctance of mainstream outlets, especially vernacular language papers and television channels, to acknowledge vigilante violence by Hindu right-wing groups. In fact, several Muslim journalists maintained that it was their outlets' reporting on hate crimes that had actually resulted in these incidents being brought to light. In this context, referencing a killing that occurred in the northern Indian state of Haryana in 2022, a journalist affiliated with Maktoob Media said:

> So, there was a lynching in Mewat last year and we called it a lynching. Initially so many media houses even NDTV said it was not a lynching... that it was a case of personal enmity...that there was no anti-Muslim angle, eventually, after a few days they reported on it as a lynching, but if we had not covered it ...

Similarly, in relation to attacks on mosques and vandalization of Muslim-owned businesses that occurred in the eastern Indian state of Tripura in 2021, another journalist from the Millat Times emphasized that it was video footage from sources on the ground obtained by his news organization (and others like it) that had been crucial to convincing local authorities that the violence had really occurred, even as Hindutva organizations and local BJP politicians sought to deny it. He pointed out that it was only later that a couple of English-language news organizations reached out to them and picked up the story (Chakrabarti, 2021).

In addition to contesting mainstream media coverage of vigilante-directed anti-Muslim violence, Muslim-run digital news media have also sought to challenge their coverage of state-sponsored violence—most notably in the BJP administered states of Uttar Pradesh, Madhya Pradesh and Gujarat—where state governments have "bulldozed" numerous Muslim-owned homes, businesses and shrines claiming that they were illegally constructed or were encroaching on public land or in some cases, because the owners were deemed to be "criminals" or accused of "rioting" (Mittal, 2023). Human rights activists have observed that not only are Muslims disproportionately affected by such actions according to Aakar Patel, chair of Amnesty International's India board, but the razing of Muslim-owned buildings is intended to "inflict punishment on the community for raising their voices," particularly as they often take place following protests or communal unrest (Mittal, 2023).

As in the case of lynchings, *mainstream news entities have* tended to either minimize these demolitions or normalize them as appropriate state responses, accepting versions of events provided by official sources who act as "primary definers of reality" (Hall et al., 1978). For example, while covering the demolition of the home of Javed Mohammad, a prominent Muslim activist who was involved in anti-BJP protests in Uttar Pradesh, mainstream news outlets not only accepted the state's claim that demolition was due to illegal construction, but the popular English-language television channel CNN News18 used provocative headlines such as "Mastermind Made to Pay," "Bulldozer Justice Time" and "Action They Won't Forget." Meanwhile, Hindi channels "zoomed in on the family's possessions and cited the presence of a poster stating "When injustice becomes law, rebellion becomes duty" as "incriminating evidence" of the activist's intent to provoke unrest while offering no context or comment from the family (Qureshi, 2022). Similarly, mainstream coverage of a demolition drive in New Delhi that targeted a Muslim neighborhood in the wake of conflict between Hindus and Muslims had "television crews, especially pro-government channels, providing breathless coverage," with the top editor of leading Hindi language channel proclaiming that "the bulldozer has become a symbol of strict legal action against illegal constructions in Indian politics, after she climbed aboard an excavator and interviewed the operator" (Shih & Gupta, 2022).

Muslim digital outlets, on the other hand, in keeping with the counter-hegemonic perspective of alternative journalism, view these events not as random, unrelated "episodes" involving routine enforcement of building codes by local authorities as typically presented by mainstream news but thematically, as reflecting broader societal trends of Muslim disenfranchisement and marginalization. Consequently, their coverage reflected in stories across multiple sites as well as in curated collections such as the Demolition Hate Tracker, video compilations on YouTube channels and documentaries such as *Erazed* (produced by *Maktoob Media*) not only situate such actions within the broader framework of Hindutva politics by highlighting the selective manner in which demolitions have been carried out in a country where illegal construction is the norm (Shih & Gupta, 2022) but also prioritize the testimony of those who have been directly affected.

Underscoring this point, the editor of the YouTube channel *Pal Pal News* emphasized that her outlet's coverage of demolitions in low-income New Delhi neighborhoods with large Muslim populations in 2022, differed from those of "godi or lap dog media who just want to poison people's minds and create an anti-Muslim agenda," stating that their reportage was based on:

Talking to the people who lived in the localities, taking their evidence seriously, the papers they show us that they are Indians not Bangladeshis as authorities claimed.

A similar focus can be seen in many stories about the abovementioned 2022 demolition of activist Javed Mohammad's house in Uttar Pradesh that feature extensive comments from his daughter Afreen Fatima (herself an activist) about the experience of witnessing the destruction of her family home (Abdulla, 2023; *Clarion India*, 2022). An example of such a story carried by *The Cognate*, quoted Afreen as follows:

My younger sister was born in that house. Our house is as old as my sister. It was like our space. We could be ourselves and be free.

(Shireen, 2023)

Such personal perspectives are also manifest in visual stories carried by Muslim news sites, which contain poignant first-person accounts from businessowners and residents whose homes and shops were—according to them—destroyed with no notice. This reliance on the subaltern sources—a defining feature of alternative journalism and a key part of the practice of Muslim-run digital news organizations—plays a crucial role in articulating a collective voice, albeit a painful one for their community.

Muslim-Produced Digital Media and Journalistic Values

With their emphasis on voice—acknowledged by numerous journalists as a primary driver for their journalism and even adopted as part of its tagline by the Muslim Mirror which defines itself as "articulating the concerns and hope of voiceless minorities and disadvantaged groups in India"—Muslim-run digital news outlets would seem to adopt what Harcup (2019) calls a "committed approach to journalism," one that implies a shift away from "the avowed practices of mainstream journalism such as balance and objectivity." With regard to this question, of where they located themselves vis-a-vis the objectivity/advocacy debate, Muslim journalists however offered mixed responses. Some argued that even as they sought to challenge what Atton (2010) has termed "dominant forms of representation" and put forth the views of their community, these efforts were conducted within the framework of professional journalism. Emphasizing this, a journalist associated with the Millat Times said:

When people alert us to an incident, either via social media or by calling us, we don't just publish claims. We do what journalists are supposed to do…we verify the stories, we try to get input from other sources on the ground like community leaders, only then we put out stories, Mainstream media accuse us of advocacy simply because they are not doing their job… they don't cover things related to our community but when we do, they get upset and claim that we are not objective.

Meanwhile, the editor of the *Muslim Mirror* plainly said, "we do our best to represent situations and events fairly, and take full care to be objective," while a founder of *Maktoob Media*—whose stated goal is to provide "hand-picked newsworthy stories focusing on human rights, minorities and policies,"—challenged the idea that his outlet was engaged in advocacy, asserting that they were simply focused on "accurately documenting the lives of marginalized people."

Other journalists interviewed, however, took a different approach to objectivity in that even as they acknowledged the importance of objectivity as a journalistic value, they simultaneously deemed it unworkable in the challenging professional context in which they operated. Making this point, a veteran Muslim journalist who had also worked in the mainstream media said:

We try to pursue objectivity, however, sometimes we end up only expressing our point of view on an issue because that is all we have access to. In political stories particularly, the BJP will not speak to Muslim reporters. We can't get to the source.

A similar observation was also reiterated by a young freelancer who said that as a hijab-wearing Muslim woman, politicians often refused to talk to her. As she said:

We like to bring both sides of the story. If there is communal violence for example, we want to get both sides on the record. But the problem is that when we go to the other side, the BJP or Hindutva groups, they won't talk to people who are visible Muslims like me or someone who has a Muslim name…they won't even give us a soundbite.

Yet other Muslim journalists—paralleling the views of many young minority journalists in the United States (Harlow, 2022)—questioned the very relevance of the notion to their work that is focused on marginalized communities. In this vein, the founder of *TwoCircles.net* (who has since exited the outlet) said:

I'm a big believer that a journalist has to be an advocate. I know that a lot of journalists including Muslim ones don't agree with this. But what are we here for? Whose stories are we publishing? If I am doing a story on terror case acquittals should I go to the police? The government? And just try to balance it out? No, their version is already out there. There is a huge power imbalance in the media and so we focus on the version that is not there, the story of people whose voice is not being heard.

Similarly, the founder of *The Cognate* acknowledged that he was "very forthcoming about the fact that he was not neutral" and that whatever his outlet wrote was from the perspective of the Muslim community because "that's what I saw was lacking, and I thought that is what I need to be doing that I need to put up the voice of the community in front of the world." Meanwhile, the long-time editor of *Milli Gazette*, even as he affirmed the importance of traditional journalistic values, calling objectivity the "hallmark" of good journalism, acknowledged the difficulties of adhering to its tenets stating that:

To be objective when lies are spread and a community is unjustly criminalized as part of a well-laid political agenda. It is difficult to be objective when issues of life and death are involved. It is difficult to be objective when your people are raped, burnt or killed in riots. It is difficult to be objective when people are lynched for alleged consumption of beef or in fake love jihad cases.

Instead, in contemporary India, he said that "objectivity" was "a luxury" that outlets like his could not afford.

Challenges Facing Muslim Digital News Media Producers

While approaches to the significance of objectivity as a professional value varied among the Muslim journalists interviewed, there was general consensus that producing news was a deeply challenging enterprise since most outlets experienced considerable difficulty in obtaining subscriptions or advertising revenues. Virtually every journalist reiterated that not only were businesses owned by the majority community unlikely to advertise in their outlets since their audience was primarily limited to Muslims but many argued that Muslim-owned businesses were also generally afraid to associate themselves with Muslim-produced media in India's current political climate.

Summing up this situation, a news site founder said, "it's not that we don't have some rich people but they don't want to be connected to a magazine or paper that may be outspoken about issues regarding the community. They think that if they advertise, they might attract the attention of government agencies and that could lead to investigations or probes and you know businessmen don't want to take that type of risk." As a result, journalists said, it was difficult to hire adequate staff, requiring them to find workarounds whether by using volunteers or freelancers. Others also pointed to threats from vigilante groups as well as the government, with several reporters referencing the arbitrary use of the Unlawful Activities Prevention Act to arrest journalists affiliated with Muslim outlets, thereby silencing them. Nevertheless, the general sentiment among Muslim digital outlets was in favor of persevering, despite challenging circumstances, to produce alternative journalism that enabled the community to resist what one reporter termed "pervasive conditions of social, political and economic alienation." As he stated bluntly, "we have to continue to do what we are doing…it is the only way for our community to retain a sense of self, to have a voice…."

Notes

1 For instance, Inqilab, the most-widely circulated Urdu daily is owned by the Jagaran Prakshan group, publisher of *Dainik Jagran*, India's most popular Hindi-language paper.

2 Language spoken in the south Indian state of Kerala.

3 Islam first came to India in the early 7th century when Arab forces came to Sindh in the lower Indus valley and established an Indo-Islamic state used in the region but Islamic presence in the sub-continent remained limited for the next 250 years.

4 Love jihad refers to a common conspiracy theory which holds that Muslim men are engaged in a concerted effort to marry and convert Hindu women.

5 The India Spend Hate Crimes Tracker is no longer in operation.

6 A term used to denote local vigilante groups usually affiliated with Hindu right-wing organizations.

7 Mindich (1998) points out that lynching-related coverage in the 19th and early 20th centuries U.S. newspapers did not question the morality of vigilante justice but focused instead on the reasons that prompted it.

References

Abdulla, S. (2023, June 11). Student leader Afreen Fatima marks one year since her home bulldozed, father's arrest. *Maktoob Media.* https://maktoobmedia.com/features/student-leader-afreen-fatima-marks-one-year-since-her-home-bulldozed-fathers-arrest/

Agha, E. (2022, March 13). Dial M for Media: New Muslim Voices. *Justice News.* https://www.justicenews.co.in/dial-m-for-media-the-new-muslim-voice/

Ahmad, S. (2022, November 25). Meet Naziya and Shabrun, two Muslim nurses from Bihar awarded by President Murmu for meritorious service. *TwoCircles.net.* https://twocircles.net/2022nov25/447511.html

Akins, H. (2020). The Indian Citizenship (Amendment) Act. United States Commission on International Religious Freedom. https://www.uscirf.gov/sites/default/files/2020%20Legislation%20Factsheet%20-%20India_0_0.pdf

Alavi, S. U. R. (2019, July 18). Shameful role of Hindi newspapers in spreading lawlessness, mob violence and hate crimes: How can goons be termed 'gau rakshak' or gau bhakt'? *IndianMuslim.com.* http://www.anindianmuslim.com/2019/07/shameful-role-of-hindi-newspapers-in.html

Ali, A. (2018, July 12). What lynchings in the 19th century US can teach us about the 'New India.' *The Wire.* https://thewire.in/communalism/lynching-19th-century-america-new-india

Amnesty International (2018). Halt the hate. https://sikhsiyasat.net/wp-content/uploads/2019/10/Halt-The-Hate-KeyFindings-Amnesty-International-India-1.pdf

Atton, C. (2010). Alternative journalism: Ideology and practice. In S. Allan (Ed.), *Routledge companion to news and journalism* (pp. 169–178). Routledge.

Bhardwaj, A. (2021, December 21). NCRB stopped collecting data on lynching, hate crime as it was 'unreliable', govt tells LS. *The Print.* https://theprint.in/india/governance/ncrb-stopped-collecting-data-on-lynching-hate-crime-as-it-was-unreliable-govt-tells-ls/785201/

Bhat, P., & Chadha, K. (2022). The mob, the state and harassment of journalists via Twitter in India. *Digital Journalism.* https://doi.org/10.1080/21670811.2022.2134164

Bhattacharya, A. (2023). Kolkata's Zakaria Street: The taste of community in the face of communal polarization. *Maktoob Media.* https://maktoobmedia.com/latest-news/kolkatas-zakaria-street-the-taste-of-community-in-the-face-of-communal-polarisation/

Chacko, P. (2018). The right turn in India: Authoritarianism, populism and neoliberalization. *Journal of Contemporary Asia.* doi: 10.1080/00472336.2018.1446546

Chadha, K., & Kavoori, A. (2008). Exoticized, marginalized and demonized: The Muslim as other. In A. Kavoori & A. Punthambekar (Eds.), *Global Bollywood.* New York University Press.

Chadha, K. (2018). From caste to faith: Contemporary identity politics in a globalized India. *Journalism and Communication Monographs, 20* (1), 84–87.

Chakrabarti, A. (2021, November 18). Tripura mosque attacks: Ground report on what really happened during those 8 days in October. *The Print.* https://theprint.in/india/tripura-mosque-attacks-ground-report-on-what-really-happened-during-those-8-days-in-october/767110/

Chakraborty, A. (2017, June 27). Those upset about India being called Lynchistan are just as complicit. *DailyO.* https://www.dailyo.in/politics/lynching-mobs-junaid-nowhatta-beef-gau-rakshak-modi-18057

Chatterjee, A. (2017). *Margins of citizenship: Muslim experiences in urban India.* Routledge.

Clarion India (2021, August 21). Muslim contribution to freedom struggle remembered. *Clarion India.* https://clarionindia.net/iamc-celebrates-indias-75th-independence-day-muslim-contribution-to-freedom-struggle-remembered/

Clarion India (2022, June 17). Demolition of Muslim homes is illegal 'collective punishment,' says activist Afreen Fatima. *Clarion India.* https://clarionindia.net/demolition-of-muslim-homes-is-illegal-collective-punishment-says-activist-afreen-fatima/

Cognate News Desk (2023, February 27). Muslim inventions that shaped the modern world. *The Cognate.* https://thecognate.com/muslim-inventions-that-shaped-the-modern-world/

Couldry, N. (2010). *Why voice matters.* Sage Publications.

Dey, A. (2017, December 30). India is undercounting religious hate crimes by failing to invoke a crucial section of the law. *Scroll.in.* https://scroll.in/article/863176/2017-india-is-undercounting-religious-hate-crimes-by-not-invoking-a-crucial-section-of-the-law

Drabu, O. (2018). Who is the Muslim? Discursive representations of the Muslims and Islam in Indian prime-time news. *Religions, 9*(9). https://www.mdpi.com/2077-1444/9/9/283

Fatima, N. (2023, May 31). Young trailblazer Maryam Mirza ignites a reading revolution with 31 mohalla libraries in Aurangabad. *TwoCircles.net.* https://twocircles.net/2023may31/449054.html

Ghosh, R. (2022, August 14). As Islamophobia infects Indian newsrooms, Muslim journalists persevere amid the bigotry. *Article 14.* https://article-14.com/post/as-islamophobia-infects-indian-newsrooms-muslim-journalists-persevere-amid-the-bigotry–62fc4b4738535

Hall, S., Critcher, C., Jefferson, T., Clarke, J., & Roberts, B. (1978). Policing the crisis: Mugging, the state and law and order. Macmillian.

Hall, S. (1981). The whites of their eyes: Racist ideologies and the media. In P. Gilroy & R. W. Gilmore (Eds.), *Selected Writings on Race and Difference* (pp. 97–120). Duke University Press. https://doi.org/10.2307/j.ctv1hhj1b9.11

Hall, S. (Ed.). (1997). *Representation: Cultural representations and signifying practices.* Sage Publications.

Hallin, D. (1986). *Vietnam: The uncensored war.* University of California Press.

Harcup, T. (2019). Alternative journalism. In J.F. Nussbaum (Ed.), *Oxford Research Encyclopaedia of Communication.* Oxford University Press. https://oxfordre.com/communication/display/10.1093/acrefore/9780190228613.001.0001/acrefore-9780190228613-e-780?d=%2F10.1093%2Facrefore%2F9780190228613.001.0001%2Facrefore-9780190228613-e-780&p=emailAWzyKly00HHgU

Harlow, S. (2022). Journalism's change agents: Black lives matter,#Blackout Tuesday, and a shift towards doxa. Journalism and Mass Communication Quarterly, 99(3), 742–762.

Human Rights Watch (2019, February, 18). India: Cow vigilante groups attack Muslims. https://www.hrw.org/news/2019/02/19/india-vigilante-cow-protection-groups-attack-minorities

Hussain. S. Z., & ul Haleem, J. (2023, September 20). Moulvi Muhammad Baqir: Freedom struggle's first journalist martyr. *The Cognate*. https://thecognate.com/moulvi-muhammad-baqir-freedom-struggles-first-journalist-martyr/

Iyer, A. (2022, October 29). As Hindutva has grown so have websites reporting on India's embattled Muslims. *Scroll.in* https://scroll.in/article/1035586/as-hindutva-has-grown-in-india-so-have-websites-reporting-on-the-plight-of-embattled-muslims

Jaffrelot, C. (1996). *The Hindu nationalist movement in India*. Columbia University Press.

Jain, K. (2023, June 7). How India's Modi has extended Hindu nationalist sway over the country's media. Religion News Service. https://religionnews.com/2023/06/07/how-indias-modi-has-extended-hindu-nationalist-sway-over-the-countrys-media/

Javeed, A. (2018, November 30). Meet Dr. Mubeena Ramzan, the first Kashmiri woman to feature among world's 500 most influential Muslims. *Two Circles.net*. https://two-circles.net/2018nov30/427436.html

Kaviraj, S. (1995). Religion, politics and modernity. In U. Baxi & B. Parekh (Eds.), *Crisis and change in contemporary India* (pp. 295–316). Sage Publications.

Khan, S. (2020). Social exclusion of Muslims in India and Britain. *Journal of Social Inclusion Studies, 6*(1), 56–77.

Khan, M. G. (2022, March 11). Lost: An India where my Pathaan daadi was mother to our next-door neighbor Mrs. Sharma. *Milli Gazette*. https://www.milligazette.com/news/Opinions/33987-lost-an-india-where-my-pathaan-daadi-was-mother-to-her-next-door-neighbour-mrs-sharma/

Khilnani, S. (1997). *The idea of India*. Penguin.

Liyakat, M. (2017). Image of Muslims in mainstream English dailies of India: A critical analysis of four major newspapers during 2007 & 2017. *IMPACT: International Journal of Research in Humanities, Arts and Literature, 5*(8), 87–100.

Maktoob Staff (2023, June 17). Nusrat Jahan Choudhury becomes first Muslim woman to be federal judge in US. *Maktoob Media*. https://maktoobmedia.com/world/nusrat-jahan-choudhury-becomes-first-muslim-woman-to-be-federal-judge-in-us/

Mander, H. (2018, November 13). New hate crime tracker in India finds victims are predominantly Muslims, perpetrators Hindus. *The Scroll*. https://scroll.in/article/901206/new-hate-crime-tracker-in-india-finds-victims-are-predominantly-muslims-perpetrators-hindus

Mattoo, F., & Shabir, S. (2023, May 20.) Kashmir's Farhat Siddique, trailblazing female theatre artist, seeks support amidst struggles. *Maktoob Media*. https://maktoobmedia.com/india/kashmirs-farhat-siddique-trailblazing-female-theatre-artist-seeks-support-amidst-struggles/

MG Correspondent (2022, January 14). Alipatta Jameela: A path breaker. *Milli Gazette*. https://www.milligazette.com/news/1-community-news/33970-alippatta-jameela-a-path-breaker/

Mindich, D. T. Z. (1998). *Just the facts. How "objectivity" came to define American journalism*. New York University Press.

Millat Times Staff (2021, November 6). Artist Shah Abul Faiz from Jamia Millia Islamia displays his new series of paintings. *Millat Times*. https://millattimes.com/

artist-shah-abul-faiz-from-jamia-millia-islamia-displays-his-new-series-of-paintings-on-mystics-and-whirling-dervishes-in-international-group-show-of-art-exhibition/

Mittal, T. (2023, April 14). The demolition of dissent in India. Coda. https://www.codastory.com/authoritarian-tech/india-bulldozers-muslim-neighborhoods/

Mujtaba, S.A. (2022, October 29). Only 3% Muslims in Indian national media. *Muslim Mirror*. https://muslimmirror.com/eng/muslims-are-only-3-in-indian-national-media/

Mujtaba, S. S. (2023, June 10). Burqa-Clad auto driver defies norms in Chennai. *Two-Circles.net*. https://twocircles.net/2023jun10/449105.html

Muslim Mirror Staff (2023, June 16). US Senate confirms first female Muslim federal judge. *Muslim Mirror*. https://muslimmirror.com/eng/us-senate-confirms-first-female-muslim-federal-judge/

Nadaf, A. H. (2021). Discursive representation of the Article 370 abrogation: A comparative CDA of the headlines of two major Indian online news publications. *Journalism, 24*(6), 1342–1361.

Navarro, L. (2010). Islamophobia and sexism: Muslim women in the western mass media. *Human Architecture: Journal of the Sociology of Self-Knowledge, 8*, 95–112.

Nizaruddin, F. (2021). Role of public WhatsApp groups within the Hindutva ecosystem of hate and narratives of "Corona Jihad." *International Journal of Communication, 15*, 1102–1119.

Qureshi, A. (2022). Indian media gloats as Muslim activist's house reduces to rubble. *Maktoob Media*. https://maktoobmedia.com/india/indian-media-gloats-as-muslim-activists-house-reduces-to-rubble/

Raghuram, S. (2011, October 31). Media is diverting attention and dividing people. *Churumuri blog*. https://churumuri.blog/2011/10/31/media-is-diverting-attention-dividing-people/

Raj, K., & Jafri, A. (2023). How Indian media mainstreamed the 'Land Jihad' propaganda. *Article 14* https://article-14.com/post/mainstreaming-of-the-land-jihad-propaganda-by-the-indian-media–6413ec7be7d2d

Raj, S. (2023, April 6). New Indian textbooks purged of Muslim history and Hindu extremism. *New York Times*. https://www.nytimes.com/2023/04/06/world/asia/india-textbooks-changes.html

Ricoeur, P. (1984). *Oneself as another* (translated by Kathleen Blamey). Chicago University Press.

Robb, P. (2002). *A history of India*. Palgrave MacMillan.

Shabir, S. (2023, May 24). Meet Mubeena Ramzan, the trailblazer in imparting women's education and property rights. *TwoCircles.net*. https://twocircles.net/2023may24/449020.html

Shih, G., & Gupta, A. (2022, April 23). How bulldozers in India became a symbol of Hindu nationalism. *The Washington Post*. https://www.washingtonpost.com/world/2022/04/27/india-hindus-muslims-bulldozers-demolitions/

Shireen, R. (2022, June 16). We are not willing to shed a single tear: Afreen Fatima on demolition of her House and incarceration of her father. *The Cognate*. https://thecognate.com/we-are-not-willing-to-shed-a-single-tear-afreen-fatima-on-demolition-of-her-house-and-incarceration-of-her-father/

Shireen, R. (2023, August 15). Contribution of Muslims to India's Freedom Struggle. *The Cognate*. https://thecognate.com/contribution-of-muslims-to-indias-freedom-struggle/

Sikander, Z. (2021). Islamophobia in Indian media. *Journal of Islamophobia Studies, 6*(2), 120–129. https://www.scienceopen.com/hosted-document?doi=10.13169/islastudj.6.2.0120

Sikdar, S. (2023, April 12). Pledge of economic boycott of Muslims, Christians administered during Monday's Chhattisgarh bandh. *The Hindu.* https://www.thehindu.com/latest-news/pledge-of-economic-boycott-of-muslims-christians-administered-during-mondays-chhattisgarh-bandh/article66729778.ece

Varshney, A. (2002). *Ethnic conflict and civic life: Hindus and Muslims in India.* Yale University Press.

Vasudevan, K. (2019). Taxi Drivers as reporters: Studying the distinctive journalism of the UTCC Voice newsletter. *Journalism Studies.* https://doi.org/10.1080/1461670X.2019.1601028

Wani, S. (2023, June 12). Erasure of Muslim intellectuals in Indian academia. *Maktoob Media.* https://maktoobmedia.com/opinion/erasure-of-muslim-intellectuals-in-indian-academia/

4 Online Citizen Journalism

Re-Imagining Journalism and Facilitating Participation in Rural India

Rakesh Rai is reporting from the Pampapur village of Surguja district in the state of Chhattisgarh. He is with a farmer Pitbasu who should be a show case person for the NREGA program because Pitbasu has completed 100 days of work in NREGA. But the story of Pitbasu is a cruel one. He has not been paid for even a single day's work so far.

(Rai, 2011)

Sheila Devi from Makhdumpur Panchayat said that the girl's toilet in her village's school was kept locked and this was posed a problem for students. She reports on how she organized a women's group to raise the issue with local authorities and eventually succeeded in getting the facility unlocked for the girls' use.

(Gram Vaani.org, n.d.)

Introduction

These are just two examples of stories produced by rurally-based and focused reporting initiatives that have emerged as the dominant form of citizen journalism in India. As a term, citizen journalism has been "used to describe the involvement of nonprofessionals in the creation, analysis, and dissemination of news and information in the public interest" (Roberts, 2019). While sometimes this involvement of citizens in journalism can "conventional and subject to the filters and processes of professional journalism," especially in contexts where ordinary people are affiliated with participatory media initiatives that are run by professional news organizations, citizen journalism also often represents "opposition" to the institutionalized press (Roberts, 2019). As such, citizen reporting can be understood as constituting a form of alternative journalism that seeks to combat what Carroll and Hacket (2006) describe as "the democratic deficits inherent in a corporate-dominated, highly commercialized media system" (p. 83). And while the nature and manifestations of such journalism can vary significantly depending on the context in which they operate: for instance, citizen journalism initiatives in the Global North often look quite different from those in the developing world where they tend to be associated with community media and communication for development (Fforde, 2019),

DOI: 10.4324/9781003244202-4

generally speaking, citizen journalism involves individuals coming together to create their own media in order to voice their under-reported news and perspectives (Atton, 2012).

That is to say, alternative/citizens journalism tends to emerge whenever non-mainstream groups contest existing societal discourses (Bosch, 2008). Generally, citizen-based alternative journalism forms, which are also sometimes described as "community media," "citizen's media" or "civil society media" (Allan & Hintz, 2019), tend not only to be situated outside dominant power structures but share certain "enduring characteristics," notably a focus on "local news or news immediately relevant to their specific audience over other news…which may in many cases lead to the breakdown of the audience-producer barrier," "provide information designed to motivate and activate citizenship" and "choose stories that fill the gaps in information coming from dominant media" (Fforde, 2019 p. 296). In addition to these defining features (that citizen journalism shares with alternative journalism more generally), the former is also typically marked by a "grassroots orientation, while being predicated on a profound sense of dissatisfaction with mainstream media form and content, dedicated to the principles of free expression and participatory democracy, and committed to enhancing community relations and promoting community solidarity" (Howley, 2005, p. 2).

Historically, the origins of modern citizen journalism can be traced back to local community owned and managed radio stations that emerged all over the world during the early 20th century. Constituting an early form of participatory media, these stations were run by amateurs who sought to employ radio technologies to develop programming in interactive, non-institutional settings. But it was the transition to digital technologies which enabled the emergence of a "citizen-designed, citizen-controlled worldwide communications network" (Rheingold, 1993, p. 15) that significantly amplified citizen journalism. Indeed, as ordinary people came to employ various web-based tools to engage in the production and dissemination of news, "the evolving interactivities of media participation, in general, and citizen-centered forms of journalism, in particular, assumed even greater resonance" (Allan & Hintz, 2019, p. 438). An early example of the phenomenon was Indymedia's crowd-sourced coverage of the Seattle WTO summit and related protests in 1999 which "aimed at representing demonstrators' perspectives and provide a different account of the protests from what was reported in traditional media" via an "open publishing" system" (Allan & Hintz, 2019, p. 439). Other widely acknowledged pivotal moments include the subsequent emergence of the Korean site *OhmyNews* in 2002 as well as user generated contributions in crisis situations such as the 2004 Asian tsunami and the 2005 London bombings when photographs and videos taken by ordinary people found their way into mainstream news coverage (Allan, 2009). Also included in this list of early exemplars of citizen journalism initiatives was WikiLeaks which like Indymedia was driven by a critique of traditional media approaches and emerged as "a prominent model of citizen journalism from 2006" (Allan & Hintz, 2019, p. 439).

Early Forms of Online Citizen Journalism in India: An Urban Bias

In the Indian sub-continent, online citizen journalism gained prominence during the early 2000s when ordinary citizens began to use new digital technologies to document and record various crisis situations. Operating as "para" citizen journalists—as per Carpenter's typology—who come to the fore in "crisis or conflict situations coalescing around an event and contributing items of news and information related to it," (Carpenter, 2019), these individuals gained prominence during the massive rain storm and subsequent floods that affected Mumbai in 2005. This event which overwhelmed the city, according to Sonwalkar (2009) not only resulted in the production of numerous eyewitness accounts and updates from residents of the city who then played a critical role in providing news and information about the crisis to online news portals such as *Rediff.com* but also signaled the rise of internet-based citizen journalism in India (p. 78). A few years later, citizen journalism once again came to the fore during the 2008 terror attacks in Mumbai when user generated content on Twitter and Flickr became important sources of news often beating mainstream news outlets whose journalists were unable to gain access to the site of the attack (Noor, 2013; Sonwalkar, 2009).

Aside from their original emergence almost exclusively in response to "crisis situations" such as natural disasters and terrorism where ordinary people who were already on the scene engaged in "witnessing" ongoing "events," citizen journalism efforts in India also gradually developed—in line with other media contexts—as a response to shortcomings in the country's mainstream media environment. As Bruns (2010) has argued, the rise of citizen journalism can be understood as a response to the inadequacies of whether "caused by a limited understanding of complex specialist topics... or a systemic and deliberate avoidance of controversial themes for political or economic reasons." This, he suggests, engendered the rise of "Internet-enabled practices of engaging with the news" that were "led not by professional journalists and editors, but by individuals and groups who often volunteered their time because of a deeply-felt belief that the coverage available from conventional news media was inadequate or biased," and consequently "sought to critique, supplement and even supplant traditional news sources" (Bruns, 2016, p. 32).

Arguably, in the Indian case, the market imperatives that came to characterize mainstream commercial media following the economic liberalization of the 1990s led news outlets to prioritize advertiser-friendly content and engage in a general "dumbing down" of content with an inordinate emphasis on covering "the three Cs" represented by "cinema, crime and cricket" (Thussu, 2007). The result was a pervasive failure to focus on substantive societal concerns that led to the rise of several citizen-based news sites. Significant among these was *merinews.com* or My News[1] that came into existence around 2006. Describing itself as "India's First Citizen Journalism News Portal," the site's motto called for "Power to the People" in a manner resonant of the South Korean *OhmyNews*, which was established in 2002 as a counterweight to conservative media outlets and published articles written by ordinary citizens under the tagline "every citizen is a reporter" (Allan, 2009). The main goal of *merinews* according to its founder Vipul Kant Upadhyay, was to create "a product with a mission: a people's news platform, of the people, by the people, for the people, providing power to the people and empowering democracy" (Sonwalkar, 2009, p. 79).

In terms of its founding statement, the site thus seemed to echo the beliefs of early advocates of citizen journalism such as Bowman and Willis (2003) who argued that citizen journalism involved "a citizen, or group of citizens, playing an active role in the process of collecting, reporting, analyzing, and disseminating news and information, in order to provide the independent, reliable, accurate, and wide-ranging and relevant information that a democracy requires" (p. 9). As an outlet, *merinews* carried contributions from everyday people including on "socially relevant beats" such as rural development, education and health that received minimal coverage in mainstream newsrooms (Sonwalkar, 2009), albeit with the caveat that contributors follow ethical practices (Roberts & Steiner, 2012). It also made a case for a different type of journalism stating that:

> Unlike regular journalism with its publishing deadlines and the determination for "complete stories" collaborative citizen journalists using blogs can develop or examine a story one piece at a time, often updating a developing story day. The participating citizens can also debate, question and further develop their own findings in an ongoing way.
>
> (merinews.com, quoted in Thomas (2012))

By highlighting issues pertaining to different segments of society, the site also sought to "reinvigorate" citizen participation in public life. In laying claim to such a goal, *Merinews* was arguably quite forward-looking. As many subsequent studies have found, citizen journalism activities such as writing news stories not only have direct and positive implications for civic participation (Nah et al., 2017), including donating to political groups or organizations or contacting politicians and public officials (Ekström & Östman, 2015) but can also engender increased offline political participation (Ardèvol-Abreu & Gil de Zúñiga, 2020). As Nah and Yamamoto (2020) put it, "involvement in news production enables citizens to be more aware of, interested in, and knowledgeable about community issues and common interests, thus motivating them to participate in civic activities individually or collectively" (p. 5179).

The establishment of *merinews.com* was followed by the emergence of a variety of other independent citizen journalism sites (*Cplash, World SnapNews, Viewspaper* and *Purdasfash News*) as well as numerous citizen journalism news blogs (*CitizenjournalistofIndia, GroundReport, Citizensreport.in* and *Pen Pricks*), which involved "ordinary people actively participate[ing] in the process of news," employing a "'broad' range of practices" (Kern & Nam, 2009, p. 641). Around the same time, several professional news outlets also encouraged readers and viewers to engage with them by sharing various types of user generated content such as text messages, photos or videos (Noor, 2013).

Most of these initiatives fell into the category of so-called participatory journalism, defined as situations where citizen journalists "contribute to traditional news organizations but have limited collaboration with professional journalists who continue to be gatekeepers and determine production norms and practices" (Carpenter, 2019). In one especially notable example of participatory journalism at the time, the news channel *CNN-IBN* set up a (now defunct) microsite entirely dedicated to the practice of citizen journalism. Here, users could share stories and express opinions, some of which were later compiled and broadcast on the television channel's *The Citizen Journalist Show: Be the Change* (exchange4media Staff, 2007). In terms of content, the site—identified at the time as one of the most visible manifestations of citizen journalism in India (Sonwalkar, 2009)—was dominated by the coverage of three major categories of issues (Noor, 2013). These were (i) the failures of public agencies to adequately carry out their duties; (ii) instances of corruption and (iii) violations of the law including by authorities, that were observed by citizens "engaged in so-called sousveillance or watching from below, motivated by the desire to remain vigilant against the excesses of the powers that be" (Hoffman, 2006).

Moreover, in line with research which suggests that citizen journalists not only vary from professional journalists in terms of news judgement but also take a different approach to story selection, language use and sourcing (see for instance, Carpenter, 2008; 2009; Kaufhold et al., 2010), Noor (2013) found that citizens on the *CNN-IBN* citizen journalism site tended to focus on issues and stories that were drawn from and relevant to their hyperlocal contexts rather than employing the standards of newsworthiness that characterize mainstream news items. In her words:

> Citizen journalists are more curious to report about the grave and hidden issues that lie right under their nose... They highlight the issues confronting them more than the issues that often hog the headlines in mainstream media. They are keener to highlight official apathy towards their plight in their vicinity than political drama elsewhere... Violation of traffic and other rules in public, especially on the part of police officials and other law enforcers, is what citizen journalists are actually concerned about rather than gossip of the entertainment world or records being broken in sports.
>
> (Noor, 2013, p. 64)

Additionally, Noor's study found that stories posted on the CNN-IBN site were often quite impactful, resulting in the resolution of myriad local grievances, leading her to call for other established news organizations to develop citizen journalism stating that "such initiatives will help common masses highlight the issues concerning them that are otherwise and often missed by the mainstream media. They can also help them bring change for better. Citizen journalism initiatives by established news organizations can have more impact than less popular organizations" (p. 65).

This period also saw the introduction of citizen journalism initiatives by several other news organizations such as *NDTV* and *MTV India* that sought to integrate viewer input and perspectives into their programming (Sonwalkar, 2009), albeit in a limited and hybrid form with professional journalists continuing to act as gatekeepers, moderating, shaping and filtering citizen-generated content. And at this particular juncture, it did seem that the practice of citizen journalism in India appeared to observers to be "generating hope that it could enrich the public sphere; enable expression of a wide range of opinions, including those of the marginalized; and expose corruption, human rights violations, and sexual harassment" (Chadha & Steiner, 2015, p. 709). Indeed, the idea that citizen journalism initiatives significantly enhance the public sphere has been frequently reiterated by its supporters, with scholars offering a range of arguments. These include claims that such initiatives enable community members to connect through engaging in conversations and collaborations with one another, allow communities to benefit from the so-called wisdom of the crowd and enable "citizens to participate in activities that further their engagement with their communities (Friedland & Rojas, n.d.).

However, the efflorescence of citizen journalism initiatives in the urban Indian context ultimately proved to be brief. Institutionally driven efforts such as the *CNN-IBN* microsite experiment gradually evaporated while an analysis of *Merinews.com* conducted in 2010 found that not only did the site's layout and sections imitate those of legacy news outlets but that the stories in various sections were themselves "mainstream" in nature. The study also found that while the site certainly contained a section for citizen reporting, it appeared that it accepted "articles on all types of issues from citizens," making it difficult to discern whether the site was "a space for inclusive deliberations on key issues facing the nation," or if was just "another channel for middle-class opinion making" (Thomas, 2012, p. 157). A more recent search for *Merinews. com* indicates the absence of any posts after 2011—indicating that the site is no longer being updated. The same is true of most of the other digital citizen journalism projects that emerged in the early 2000s in urban India but now appear to be inactive. This is not surprising given that citizen journalism projects in general tend to be short-lived. Indeed, as Friedland and Rojas point out, "sustaining a distributed enterprise requires time, attention, and skill, from both producers and contributors/readers" (Friedland & Rojas, n.d.), and this typically proves challenging either due to shifting institutional priorities as in the case of participatory journalism projects or changes in group cohesion or motivation and interest in the case of community members.

But aside from such structural issues, citizen journalism initiatives have arguably also been impacted by the rise of social media. Even though some scholars view social media as heralding the "second wave of citizen journalism" (Bruns, 2015) and suggest that citizens on such platforms demonstrate far greater participation in the "crucial journalistic activities of reporting, evaluation and dissemination" than were manifest in the early stand-alone exemplars of citizen journalism, the phenomenon in the sense of active involvement by ordinary people in news production by "gathering content, visioning, producing and publishing the news product" (Abbott, 2017) currently seems to have relatively little purchase as either idea or practice at least in the Global North. Roberts (2019), for example, asserts that many of the once intense debates about the nature, scope and significance of citizen journalism as a practice and its contested relationship to professional journalism, appear to have "lost steam." Instead, according to her, the phenomenon of citizen journalism is being "subsumed into the vast amounts of sharing that takes place on social media, where citizens sharing information has become commonplace." This state which characterizes much of the developed world, is also largely true of urban India, where citizen journalism initiatives have been largely overtaken by engagement with social media platforms.

Contemporary Forms of Online Citizen Journalism in India: The Rural Turn

But even as online citizen journalism projects have generally waned in the context of India's metropolitan centers where they had initially emerged, barring rare episodes like the 2015 Chennai rains when residents of the city "committing random acts of journalism" played a key role in relaying news as it happened including to mainstream outlets (Nath, 2015), such initiatives nevertheless continue to have a meaningful presence in different parts of rural India. This trend is similar to other parts of the Global South where according to Mutsvairo and Salgado (2022), "citizen journalism…has maintained a noticeable presence even though it has apparently nose-dived elsewhere" (p. 355). Established variously by professional journalists, academics and non-governmental organizations working in concert with community members, these rural reporting initiatives have an interest in focusing on hyperlocal news or addressing what Carpenter (2019) calls "perceived gaps in coverage by reporting on issues overlooked by professional news organizations." In the Indian case, this absence or gap is especially evident in the fact that even though 64% of the country's population lives in rural areas, these regions remain "media dark zones" (Inamdar, 2018).

Observing this situation, Ninan (2007) has stated that although the number of rural newspaper editions in India has increased since the early 2000s, not only does their coverage lean toward the "trivial" but news organizations tend to be concerned with increasing market share and display little interest in providing a public sphere for rural issues. Similarly, Mudgal (2011) found that 98% of the coverage of India's top Hindi and English language dailies was focused on urban areas, with a mere 2% being devoted to rural issues. Meanwhile, according to Murthy (2015), although the Indian state had made some initial efforts to provide relevant programming to rural areas in the post-independence period via state-controlled broadcasting, the deregulation of India's television sector in the 1990s had created a "dismal" situation with commercial national television channels offering little rural-focused content. Summarizing the overall state of reporting on rural issues, one media observer recently wrote:

> It is quite apparent that rural journalism remains a grey area in Indian journalism. Journalists working in urban areas are not nuanced enough to understand and report rural problems. The paucity of reporters at grassroots level, less space or time allocation, and shoddy newsroom management have further damaged rural journalism… Unfortunately, the empowering role of journalism has been weakened as priority is being given to making profits.
> (Biswal, 2018)

Arguably it is such failures of mainstream news organizations to address what scholars term the "critical information needs" of rural communities that have emerged as a significant driver for community-based reporting initiatives. These projects—that gather and disseminate news leveraging the growing penetration of mobile telephony and internet in rural India[2]—seek to engage local residents and encourage them to participate in news production with a distinct orientation toward serving the public interest. Notable among these citizen journalism projects are *CGNet Swara*, *Gram Vaani*, and *Video Volunteers* (VV). These initiatives differ in terms of the geographic areas that they cover as well as the manner in which they are organized and engage with rural communities. Nevertheless, they are united by the fact that they all focus on marginalized communities and appear to hew closely to definitions of citizen journalism, which hold that citizen journalism is: "not produced by a traditional news organization; is produced by a group, and strives to cover marginalized communities through recruitment of members of these communities and coverage of these communities" (Rutigliano, 2008).

For instance, *CGNet Swara*—the oldest of these initiatives—initially came into being in 2004 as *CGNet*,[3] a website and listserv aimed at focusing on rural, tribal or Adivasi communities in the central Indian state of Chhattisgarh. Comprising about 30% of the region's population, these communities experience both consistent violation of their rights—both human and economic—and poverty rates almost double those of the rest of the country having been "continually excluded from the nation's idea of development" (Philip & Dutta, 2022). Moreover, Chhattisgarh—which has

Figure 4.1 Screenshot of *CGNet Swara* website, the oldest rural online journalism site in India.

been the site of a long-running Maoist movement that has been described as India's most serious internal security threat—has historically received little attention from the news media except in relation to so-called Maoist "terror" (Shubhranshu Choudhary, personal communication, 2023). The establishment of *CGNet*, which was later transformed into the current voice-based *CGNet Swara* in 2010 (see Figure 4.1), came about due to the efforts of Shubhranshu Choudhary, a professional journalist who had worked in local papers and the BBC.

Choudhary, who grew up in the region, was primarily motivated by what he perceived to be the lack of meaningful representation of tribal issues in media coverage as well as the inability of these communities to put forth their concerns within the public sphere. Indeed, like many marginalized groups in India, Adivasis have long been excluded from public conversation due to endemic caste-based asymmetries of power—a fact that has obvious implications for coverage. Moreover, the situation in Chhattisgarh is further complicated by situational concerns such as the Maoist insurgency in the state that made it challenging for journalists to report on the hinterlands, along with structural limitations that also contributed to the reporting deficit. As Choudhary has put it "No journalists understand their languages, mainly Kurukh and Gondi or belong to their communities … so their views are not represented. The 95 percent are ignored," (Shubhranshu Choudhary, personal communication, 2023). However, it soon became evident that for *CGNet* to reach rural communities who lacked access to the internet at the time and were more comfortable with oral forms of communication, a new modality was necessary.

Consequently, in 2010, Choudhary decided instead to turn to mobile telephony which was becoming available even in rural areas and launched *CGNet Swara* (or Voice), a toll-free service that allowed villagers to record and receive recorded messages through a simple interactive voice response (IVR) system. IVR, according to scholars, offers an "inclusive means of accessing, reporting and sharing information in rural communities" (Marathe et al., 2015). As part of this system, callers were asked to give a "missed" call to the server by dialing the *Swara* number and hanging up while the phone was still ringing. The server then called them back immediately, prompting them to either record a story or listen to recorded stories sent in by other community members (Corsa, 2014). Originally developed to circumvent high cell phone call charges as mobile telephony was taking off in the country, the use of the so-called "missed call" was a common practice in India and by employing this practice, *CGNet Swara* was able to facilitate easy and cost-free participation from the outset (Mudliar & Donner, 2015).

While calling in and listening was and remains unmoderated, for a report to be "posted" on the IVR system for others to hear, it has—as in conventional journalistic settings—to be deemed "truthful" and "relevant to the broader community," with the additional caveat that callers show that they had already attempted to address the issue via the appropriate governmental channels (Corsa, 2014); the idea being to encourage people to participate in addressing their community problems rather than only relying on external assistance. As Devansh Mehta who directs research for the program put it, "the idea is to help people with their fight, not to fight it for them" (Devansh Mehta, personal communication, 2023). In order to ensure that reports actually meet these criteria, the recorded messages or "stories" subsequently undergo an editorial process whereby they are verified, edited and posted by cadre of volunteer editors who are typically drawn from the community and work under the supervision of the founder (Corsa, 2014). This, as the process suggests, is a time-consuming task. However, unlike conventional editorial processes at professional journalism organizations where editors decide on whether an item is considered newsworthy, here "editors are more on the technical and fact-checking side rather than acting as gatekeepers to filter through a certain type of news" (Pain et al., 2022, p. 56). The messages that make it through this process are subsequently made available for playback on the *CGNet Swara* website as well as over the IVR phone system.

In 2015, the project developed an Android application that allowed the collection and dissemination of news using Bluetooth to further its reach into areas without internet access. And recently, in yet another modification of what its founder calls the *CGNet Swara* "experiment" (Shubhranshu Choudhary, personal communication, 2023), the team also added a WhatsApp-based chatbot to *CGNet*. As a platform, WhatsApp is immensely popular in India, having been downloaded over five billion times. Since this integration, which enables the initiative "to meet users where they are," the latter can submit video stories in addition to audio clips while also being able to receive content from the project on a familiar platform (Mehta, 2021).

In order to popularize the platform, members of *CGNet*'s core team undertake "yatras" or journeys to villages in different parts of Chhattisgarh where they hold performances using a traveling dance and puppetry troupe, to spread awareness about *CGNet Swara*'s activities and encourage potential volunteers to engage with the project. These volunteers are offered a short training, following which, a small subset is selected for more intensive training as are editors and moderators of citizen generated content (Devansh Mehta, personal communication, 2023). Some of the trainees also serve as "local proponents or field champions of the service…soliciting and intermediating posts on the behalf of others" (Marathe et al., 2015). Since its inception approximately 13 years ago, *CGNet* has received over one million messages resulting in 32,825 stories according to the project's team (William Thies, personal communication, 2023).

Meanwhile, *Gram Vaani* (meaning Village Voice) emerged out of a social technology company established by Aaditeshwar Seth, a New Delhi-based computer science professor, who was interested in creating a community-oriented media platform, with the "intent of reversing the flow of information, that is, to make it bottom-up instead of top-down," (see Figure 4.2) (*Gramvaani.org*). The organization began to take shape in 2009 and after a pilot project in 2011, launched the *Mobile Vaani* platform, where similar to the *CGNet* model, rural users are able to call a toll-free number and access an IVR system that allows them to both leave messages about issues related to their communities or listen to messages left by others. As in the case of *CGNet Swara*, this platform also uses the popular "missed call concept," thereby "making the system free of cost for users," since the latter are not charged for incoming calls in India (Moitra et al. 2016). Moreover, mimicking social

Figure 4.2 Screenshot from Gram Vaani website.

media platforms—the *Mobile Vaani* system—which actually describes itself "as a social media platform equivalent to Facebook/YouTube/Twitter for rural areas" (*Gramvaani.org*)—also gives users the option to comment, like and forward messages as well as seek out content by navigating to information related to different topics on the site (Moitra et al., 2016). The goal is to use technology to create a platform that "people find accessible and adaptable" (*Gramvaani.org*).

Like *CGNetSwara*, the *Mobile Vaani* team also seeks to create networks by interacting with community leaders to "orient" them to the mission and vision of the platform as a form of community media while also identifying potential volunteers who are interested in contributing to the project. Typically, these volunteers have varying backgrounds ranging from social workers, community health workers, teachers and even local journalists who may also be employed by professional outlets (usually as stringers). In other words, they are a diverse group. The volunteers from different villages in a district are also organized into clubs so that they can interact with one another, identify significant issues, "guide and mentor new volunteers," and communicate with *Mobile Vaani*'s community managers who are part of *Gram Vaani*'s organizational structure. According to the *Gram Vaani* website, since its establishment, *Mobile Vaani* has received over 1.5 million calls, sometimes as many as 10,000 a day from unique rural users living in the states where it has a significant presence, namely the central Indian state of Madhya Pradesh and the eastern states of Bihar, Orissa and Jharkhand (*GramVaani.org*) as well as Delhi and surrounding areas.

While both *CGNet Swara* and *Gram Vaani* thus rely primarily on voice-based platforms, *Video Volunteers*—as the name suggests—is a video-focused community media organization. It was founded in 2003 by Jessica Mayberry—who had originally been involved in training rural Indian women in filmmaking—working with her partner Stalin K., a media and human rights activist and documentary film-maker. Defining itself as a human rights organization, the stated goal of VV (as it is generally known) is to facilitate the production of community media, i.e. what it calls "media for and by communities" by employing (in a literal sense) members of marginalized rural communities in India's poorest districts to engage in the production of "issue" videos aimed at authorities that enable them to highlight grievances and seek redressal. Once a problem has been "solved," those involved in bringing the issue to light are encouraged to produce an "impact" video, for which they are also paid. In this regard, VV's model is different from both that of *CGNet Swara* which does not pay participants at all and *Gram Vaani* which provides limited funds to its volunteer clubs for reporting associated costs.

VV's principal or "flagship program" *India Unheard* was established in 2010 and centers on a network of approximately 248 Community Correspondents (CCs) across 19 states, arguably giving it the largest footprint of such citizen journalism initiatives (*Video Volunteers.org*). Recruited from local communities, CCs—who like professional journalists, cannot be affiliated with political parties or hold elected office—receive journalistic training and eventually a small subset are chosen to work with the organization's network, operating mainly at the village level (Jessica Mayberry, personal communication, 2023). Community Correspondents have produced approximately 20,400 "issue" and "impact videos"[4] videos since the inception of the program (*Video Volunteers.org*).

Even though *CGNet Swara*, *Gram Vaani* and *VV* define themselves in varying ways (as a voice-based platform for citizen journalism, a social tech company and as a community media and human rights organization, respectively), together they demonstrate a shared commitment to media production as a participatory, community-focused activity. In doing so, these initiatives seem to reprise the values of the earlier development communication paradigm that came to the forefront in India in the 1970s. Emerging as a challenge to the so-called modernization framework of the 1950s and 1960s which sought to employ mass media to advocate for a specific economic and political trajectory based on the experiences of the Global North, development communication militated against the notion of a top-down model of information dissemination (Melkote & Steeves, 2001). Instead, proponents of development communication called for the flow of communication from "local communities to experts and horizontal communication flows between people" (Kaushik & Suchiang, 2022). This stance is clearly embodied by *CGNet Swara*, *Gram Vaani* and *VV*, which take as their point of departure the assumption that marginalized communities "have diverse information norms and needs which are not easily met by platforms controlled by outsiders" (Moitra et al., 2016).

As such, they differ significantly from mainstream news outlets—including those in the digital realm which despite the possibilities for collaboration offered by the affordances of the internet, tend to constrain audience involvement, confining it to the information gathering phase of online journalism, with agenda-setting power and editorial control remaining firmly in the hands of professionals (Singer et al., 2011). Indeed, even though so-called digital tools and platforms have ostensibly created a so-called "flatter" and "networked media environment" (Castells, 2009), with greater opportunities for civic participation, ordinary citizens and the content they provide more often than not tend to be treated as "material" by commercial news organizations (Ahva et al., 2019, p. 158). This is all too evident in the Indian context where despite the existence of numerous news outlets that have a significant digital presence, engagement and participation by audiences (beyond comments sections or the occasional blog post) remain limited. This is even more true in the case of marginalized rural communities whose media participation is further hindered by lack of education, technological skills as well as limitations of access.

In contrast to this ethos, the outlets discussed above seek to situate media making practices within communities, enabling people to participate directly in producing and presenting forms of "knowledge and information" that are under-represented, marginalized or ignored by other, more dominant media" (Atton, 2019). In this regard, Shubhranshu Choudhary of *CGNet Swara*—who has (among the three projects) articulated perhaps the most explicit connection between *CGNet Swara*'s activities and democratic politics stated that an "aristocratic mode of communication," which is how he described contemporary Indian media—was antithetical to democracy and that his fundamental goal was to establish an inclusive media based on popular participation in Chhattisgarh (Shubhranshu Choudhary, personal communication, 2023). Making this point, he said:

> If we want to live in a peaceful society, it is not enough for our elections to be democratic…We need for the media to be democratic as well, so that everybody, all of us, has a say in deciding what issues are going to be discussed, not just a few wealthy media proprietors and their chosen editors.
>
> (Smith, 2014)

Indeed, in his view, the ongoing Maoist insurgency—which mainstream media almost exclusively frames as terrorism against the nation state—is fundamentally linked to the inability of tribal citizens to gain redressal for their concerns. As he put it:

> I saw there were really two wars going on in Chhattisgarh…One involved a small fraction of the rebels who were fanatically committed to communism. The other involved the vast majority of their followers, mainly poor, lower-caste tribal people, who had picked up rifles and joined the Maoists because they had run out of patience. They could think of no other way to call attention to the grievances they had and the problems

they were facing—things like poverty, lack of health care, poor sanitation, crime, corruption, unpaid wages, and the fact that nobody listens to them or seems to care. It wasn't communism they wanted but to have a voice, to be heard and taken seriously.

(Smith, 2014)

According to Choudhary, *CGNet Swara* is an effort to address this deficit. And while he acknowledges that the project cannot magically "solve" all the problems faced by tribal communities, he suggests that it offers tribal communities a space where they can share report on their concerns, share information and seek solutions (Shubhranshu Choudhary, personal communication, 2023).

Relatedly, *Gram Vaani* defines its mission as challenging "socio-economic ideologies and norms that are responsible for the reproduction of all forms of inequality" by providing a community media technology platform" that aims to be "equitably accessible to people," especially those who belong to marginalized groups, help build "a shared understanding among people of matters of concern" and "facilitate action by leveraging the power of media to demand better models of change" (*GramVaani.org*, 2019). A defining characteristic of this project then is emphasis on community empowerment, based on the principle that "change needs to be demanded by the people," with media playing a critical role in mediating this process. In a similar vein, *VV* states that the organization empowers

Marginalized people to tell their stories and support change campaigns, so that their issues come out from under the rug and become important threads in a country's development narrative. We believe that marginalized citizens have as much of a right to be seen and heard as the privileged do. Today, technological advances make it possible developmental decision-making to become more inclusive and bottom up.

(Video Volunteers.org)

The organization goes underscore that:

Strong alternate voices in the media – representing a diversity of genders, cultures, castes, religions, geographies and socio-economic groups – are crucial to a vibrant democracy.

While pointing out that:

On any given day in India, only 2% of content in mainstream media addresses the issues of the rural areas, where 70% of the population lives. The media does not, yet, show us the real India.

And it seeks to remedy this situation by encouraging community-based media production which it asserts:

> Empowers those who produce it (and appear in it) with a voice; it builds the social capital of a community to address critical local issues and it gives people full control over their own narratives. And often, it communicates people's needs to authority and leads to concrete resolution of local problems.
>
> (Video Volunteers.org)

Integral to this project—according to its founders—is "the intellectual, creative, and leadership development of community media-makers; community ownership of the content creation process; solution-oriented stories; and community discussion and viewing of the content." Overall, these citizen journalism projects are thus focused on building interactions with community members that are aimed not merely at increasing their participation *in* journalism," but rather "at building effective interfaces" that enable them to undertake "participation *through* journalism (Ahva et al., 2019, p. 159).

Re-Imagining Journalism and Facilitating Participation

The choice to deploy easy to navigate IVR systems or the use of phones to record videos by VV's community correspondents arguably constitute such efforts. As Mudliar and Donner (2015) point out, technologies—as in the case of *CGNet Swara* and *Gram Vaani*—that have been "specifically selected" to allow for "greater two-way interaction between individuals and civil society" (p. 370) can be deemed participatory by their very nature, especially since they enable participation without requiring "much by way of textual or technical literacies from users" (p. 378).

Concomitantly, these initiatives also represent an attempt at "re-imagining journalism" in practice (Atton & Hamilton, 2008, p. 135) by "working with different news values," and consequently "covering a different range of subjects and giving access to and foregrounding different sets of news actors and sources" (Harcup, 2019). This is evident variously in terms of the processes of news gathering as well as the actual content itself. Indeed, though all three initiatives were initially established by individuals and groups outside rural communities and who continue to provide various forms of technological, logistical or financial support, it is the *members* of various marginalized communities who play key roles in news making with their communities as the focus of coverage.

For instance, in the case of *CGNet Swara*, according to its founder, "the first information always comes from ordinary people," who call into the system and although this information is subsequently "cross-checked and verified" (Shubhranshu Choudhary, personal communication, 2023), it is community members whose initiative provides the impetus, whether in the form of contributors or trained field champions who post on the behalf of others. Similarly, in the case of *VV*, community correspondents—drawn from traditionally underrepresented groups that live below the poverty line—are responsible for identifying and reporting on stories in their localities. In fact, according to the estimates, more than half of the community correspondents are female and close to two-thirds are members of so-called Scheduled Castes and Tribes, groups that are constitutionally recognized as marginalized (Jessica Mayberry, personal communication, 2023).

On the *Mobile Vaani* platform too, in addition to community members who call in with concerns, individuals such as village teachers or health workers are encouraged to "contribute content on topics of their specialization" (*Gram Vaani* team, personal communication, 2023). Even in the case of the organization's so-called "seeded campaigns" in which communities are encouraged to engage with certain social and economic issues relevant to their communities, the actual instances of problems that they seek to highlight are identified and articulated by individuals who reach out to the IVR system (*Gram Vaani* team, personal communication, 2023). Calls from women about their personal experiences with child marriage—a significant issue in many parts of rural India (*Gram Vaani*.org)—constitute a recent example of such campaigns. Moreover, "asynchronous conversations through voice messages where callers record their comments on messages left by other callers, much like on a mailing list or Facebook wall," (Moitra et al., 2016) serves as a major source of content. As one observer commenting on the *Mobile Vaani* platform put it:

> It is like an ideal community media platform where people represent themselves the way they want to. They don't need an external news agency or a journalist to cover their issues on their behalf... it is the people who own and run the entire MV platform right from choosing the issue they want to base their discussion on, to composing a report, a message, a song or poetry... and recording it on the forum with a view to encourage further discussion within the community or make a dent in government administration.

Thus, what would seem to be work here is what Rodriguez (2001) calls citizen's journalism where journalism is part of citizens' everyday lives and the media they produce that is driven by their motivations.

In addition to involving community members, scholars suggest that citizen-produced media "privilege the communication needs" of local communities(Quintero et al., 2015, p. 124). Meanwhile, their news production avoids the one-way communication, whereby "topics are chosen in the same way by professional communicators and targeted towards the apparent interests of the audience" (Berrigan, 1979, p. 7). In the case of *CGNet Swara*, this can mean citizen filed stories on issues such as non-working hand pumps, the absence of medical aid during a cholera epidemic or tribal workers not receiving compensation or payment under different governmental schemes as demonstrated by some of the reports featured on the platform's website. That is to say, grievances which affect individuals (such as lack of access to basic utilities, denial of entitlements or land rights or more typically, lack of access to basic utilities)—commonly referred to in India as "bijli, paani aur sadak" (or electricity, water and road) issues—comprise a major focus of the news reported. In other words, rural citizen journalists highlight situations that are symptomatic of greater institutional failure" on the part of local and regional authorities (Saha, 2012). While grievances and their resolution thus make up the most substantial component of *CGNet Swara*'s reporting, in contrast to mainstream news sites, the site also contains folk songs and other types of cultural expressions "contributed" by listeners, thus prioritizing "local aesthetics" (Quintero et al., 2015, p. 124).

Similarly, in the case of *VV*, CCs are trained to typically highlight locally salient problems. As the organization's founder put it:

> During our training we tell the correspondents that you can make issue videos on whatever you want, so long as it is a community issue and so long as you're not doing it to settle personal scores or conflicts.
>
> (Jessica Mayberry personal communication, 2023)

Consequently, typical issue-based videos featured on VV's YouTube channel focus on stories such as the lack of a girls' school in a village, the exclusion of a village from a rural electrification scheme, wage theft or the failure of village authorities to allocate funds for building toilets under a national scheme. In fact, the articulation of grievances and calls for their resolution are a significant proportion of the stories produced by both *CGNet Swara* and *VV*, even though this was not necessarily the original intent, at least in the case of the former. An early study of *CGNet Swara*, for example, found that "grievance redressal was an emergent and unexpected category of activity" (Mudliar et al., 2012), a point also corroborated by its founder, who underscored the significance of the platform's role in this regard (Shubhranshu Choudhary, personal communication, 2023). The case of *Gram Vaani* is somewhat different in the sense that although grievances made up the bulk of its "reported" content when it launched, its content has since diversified to include hyperlocal news as well as information on health, agriculture, social issues and different types of cultural expressions such as songs and poetry. According to one *Gram Vaani* team member, "80 percent of the platforms content is made up of hyperlocal updates…people who see themselves as reporters report about all sorts of news related to their areas, including about local election results, this has made *Gram Vaani* into a broader platform that appeals to different types of users (*Gram Vaani* team, personal communication, 2023).

The conceptualization of what constitutes news as reflected in the "stories" carried by these platforms is demonstrably different from the (extremely limited) rural news stories produced by mainstream Indian news outlets, which tend to be "episodically" rather than "thematically" framed, focusing on sensational stories of violence or natural disaster (i.e. events that meet commercial outlets' threshold of negativity or impact). In contrast, rural citizen reporters, who operate with different news values—though they do not refer to them as such—generally emphasize stories that are contextually relevant to them both in terms of geographic as well as cultural proximity. The result is a very different news agenda.

Moreover, in keeping with what Pajnik (2019) identifies as a "distinct characteristic of alternative journalism," namely "that it tends to avoid validating its reports by consulting economic and political elites," these platforms also prioritize sourcing that employs "the voices of activists, members of minorities or local residents" (p. 118). A recent study comparing sourcing patterns between *CGNet Swara* and the website of a regional edition of the *Times of India*—India's most widely circulated English language newspaper—found "significant differences between the sources used in the two sites for similar stories. For *CGNet Swara*, the non-official sources play a very active role being quoted over official sources and for the *Times of India*, official sources being the main spokespersons for the narratives" (Pain, 2018, p. 406). Similarly, both *VV* and *Gram Vaani* featured stories generally tend to center so-called "ordinary people" as sources, treating then in the words of Atton (2019) "as experts in their own social settings,"(p. 2)—a practice that in his view not only calls into question the manner in which mainstream news media approach sourcing but also constitutes a more ethical form of journalism.

While the community-centered efforts of *CGNet Swara*, *Gram Vaani* and *VV* have thus given rise to a demonstrably different form of journalism than that produced by professional journalists, participation in the production of news from "below" also has significant implications for rural community members in both individual and collective terms. Indeed, testimony from citizens indicates that involvement with these platforms fosters, for many, a sense of personal agency. For instance, a Dalit woman from Madhya Pradesh said that contributing to *CGNet Swara* had made her "more fearless and feeling better equipped to deal with government officials," while another participant from the same area said that filing reports on the *CGNet* IVR system made people like himself "more aware of their rights and power," which they used "to make other citizens aware of their rights (Corsa, 2014). Others said that even though reporting and posting news on *CGNet* did not always result in immediate redressal of their problems, they nevertheless felt that it was more effective than "sitting outside an officer's door for hours only to be shooed away," and as such helped to reduce the feeling of being "completely helpless" (Pain et al., 2022).

Meanwhile, a female community correspondent affiliated with *VV* noted that her work with the organization had given her a sense of confidence and self-efficacy. Explaining this she said "not only have I become better at shooting videos but I can do things on my own, not depending on people…people respect me as a community correspondent of *Video Volunteers*. Sometimes I don't need to even physically visit the officials. I have created impacts just by posting on relevant WhatsApp groups" (*Video Volunteers.org*, 2023). In this vein, another Dalit woman who has worked with *VV* for several years said:

> I always wanted to be the voice of those who are otherwise unheard. I talk to my community, understand their issues, demands and reasons. Then I work with them to get in touch with the administration and protest if need be till their problems are resolved. These are issues, even the national media ignores or doesn't highlight much.
>
> (Video Volunteers.org)

Similarly, a 21-year-old student said that engagement with stories about gender-based violence on the *Mobile Vaani* platform had encouraged her to "take up social work" and "help create a society that doesn't encourage violence against women," while another 18-year-old female student said that working with *Mobile Vaani* had "improved" her "standing in the community" because people now viewed her "as someone working towards a social cause," while yet another participant—a young mother with children—said that being able to work as a citizen journalist (Moitra et al., 2016) had:

> Helped women like me, come out of our conservative households, build our identity as community reporters and stand for ourselves for finding solutions to our problems.

Others emphasized how their work as citizen journalists empowered them in relation to the caste hierarchy that otherwise overdetermines a variety of social interactions in rural India. In this regard, an award-winning Dalit citizen journalist working with *VV* said:

> The real award, however, was the chair that I was offered[5] while visiting the homes of higher caste neighbors. This, for me is the real change. I want to capitalize on it and bring about change that is much needed in my community.
>
> (Video Volunteers.org)

At a collective level, involvement with such community media initiatives that enable citizens to highlight problems and frame their concerns as legitimate while identifying official institutions as the target of their complaints also encourages them to demand greater accountability and better governance. Such citizen-based grassroots efforts are especially important in contexts such as India where in addition to weak democratic representation, local authorities exercise considerable power while traditional accountability mechanisms such as internal monitoring and oversight tend to be inadequate (Kruks-Wisner, 2022). Learning both about the issues faced by other individuals and the manner in which they seek to resolve provides people with knowledge as well as tools and templates for action—critical in developing a sense of empowerment, however tentative. In this regard, one community correspondent working with *VV* recounted how posting an issue video on social media about the failure of a local police officer to file a report not only resulted in intervention by a senior functionary but also demonstrated to the community their ability to impact outcomes, at least to a degree. Moreover, several community correspondents also made the point that contributing to issue videos that outlined specific problems or deficits made members feel that they were capable of bringing about change. As one community correspondent based in the north Indian state, Uttar Pradesh, put it:

> When community members…see themselves in the video speaking out on a certain issue, they feel proud of themselves…I remember one of the young men who [after seeing himself] was asking everyone, wasn't I looking like a hero…
>
> (Kruks-Wisner, 2022)

Similarly, in the case of *CGNet Swara*, where participants are encouraged to both record their stories and follow up with local officials by providing relevant contact information, contributors underscored how such "activism" served to convince people that they could play a role in resolving their own problems. Elaborating on this, a contributor explained that participating in *CGNet Swara* helped community members realize that they had a "voice" and that they could "solve issues to improve their quality of life" (Marathe et al., 2015). Mirroring such sentiments, a contributor to *Mobile Vaani* highlighted how engagement with platform translated into desired outcomes. In his words:

> A few weeks back, I recorded a message about a school headmaster harassing students by charging Rs.10 per student to issue them the admit card.[6] When a few students refused to pay the amount, the headmaster threatened to fail the students in the practical exams. After my messages got published in the MV platform, it spread like wildfire. Everybody got to know about the tactics of the headmaster. So, the headmaster called a meeting of all the parents and owned up to his mistake. The headmaster promised not to repeat such a mistake in the future…
>
> (Moitra et al., 2016)

In other instances, groups have come together to exercise their communicative rights to demand and obtain redressal in varied instances of official corruption or failure to implement government mandates and policies (Shubhranshu Choudhary, personal communication, 2023; *Gram Vaani* team, personal communication, 2023).

Of course, not all efforts at citizen mobilization and participation are effective. As Atton and Hamilton (2008) point out alternative journalism is often beset by what they call "problems of voluntarism" such as the amount of time and energy that individuals can devote to such activities. Moreover, despite their efforts to implement egalitarian ways of organizing, they are not "immune to the political and economic constellations of society" (Pajnik, 2019, p. 119). While these vary across contexts, in India they tend to be manifest in imbalances of power within rural communities especially around issues of caste and gender that can impact the ability of community members to participate as well as skepticism within marginalized communities about the possibility of effecting change. However, as the accounts of numerous community members indicate participation in alternative citizen journalism projects clearly affects how they obtain information, mobilize and act in their communities—activities which in turn have broader societal effects.

Indeed, although none of the projects reference Paolo Freire, his notion of conscientização or conscientization, whereby individuals are encouraged to break through the "culture of silence," and engage in critical reflection about their living conditions and become "subjects" engaged in changing the social structures that prevent them from doing so, seems relevant here. While Freire emphasized the role of literacy and pedagogy in effecting changes in consciousness, participation in alternative journalism—which constitute a "reflexive form of activism" (Hackett & Caroll, 2006, p. 96)— arguably has similar effects in terms of effecting change. Just as dialogue enables people meet to discover reality and transform it together (Freire, 1970), efforts to identify and resolve community grievances enable individuals not only to become more aware of their agency—that is, go from being objects to subjects to use Freire's terminology—but also to acquire skills for enacting citizenship collectively in everyday life. This is not the "individualized, private and rational citizenship that is informed by the objective press" (Pajnik, 2019, p. 115) and usually expressed through voting, but rather a form of citizenship in which ordinary people actively engage in public life. By participating in citizen journalism initiatives in varied forms, whether as contributors who raise grievances and record messages on IVR systems as in the case of both *CGNet Swara* and *Gram Vaani* or as VV's community correspondents who prepare videos and interface with local authorities, individuals learn to recognize their "rights," particularly the right to demand redressal. Indeed, while such participation may not easily or irreversibly alter existing socio-political and economic structures, it does arguably create spaces in which rural communities in India can seek to challenge and re-negotiate the boundaries that otherwise define and often constrain their lives.

Notes

1 The word Meri means my in Hindi.
2 Penetration of cell phones and internet has tripled in India since 2015 and currently includes 37% of rural residents (ET Bureau, 2022). Moreover, according to recent data, by 2025, over half of all new internet users in India will be in rural areas.
3 CG refers to Central Gondwana, the region where the project operates.
4 Issue videos highlight problems while impact videos focus on their resolution.
5 Members of lower castes are typically not offered chairs and have to sit on the floor when they visit members of upper castes in many rural settings.
6 Admit cards are identification issued to students by schools as proof of identity before they can take examinations.

References

Abbott, J. Y. (2017). Tensions in the scholarship on participatory journalism and citizen journalism. *Annals of the International Communication Association, 41*(3–4), 278–297.

Ahva, L., Heikkila, H., & Kunelius, R. (2019). Civic participation and the vocabularies for democratic journalism. In C. Atton (Ed.), *The Routledge companion to alternative and community media* (pp. 155–164). Routledge.

Allan, S. (2009). Histories of citizen journalism. In S. Allan, & E. Thorsen (Eds.), *Citizen journalism: Global perspectives* (pp. 17–32). Peter Lang.

Allan, S., & Hintz, A. (2019). Citizen journalism and participation. In K. Wahl-Jorgensen, & T. Hanitzsch (Eds.), *The handbook of journalism studies* (pp. 435–451). Routledge.

Ardèvol-Abreu, A., & Gil de Zúñiga, H. (2020). "Obstinate partisanship": Political discussion attributes effects on the development of unconditional party loyalty. *International Journal of Communication, 1*, 324–345.

Atton, C. (2006). *Alternative media*. Sage.

Atton, C. (2012). Alternative journalism: Ideology and practice. In S. Allan (Ed.), *The Routledge companion to news and journalism* (pp. 169–178). Routledge.

Atton, C. (2019). Introduction. In C. Atton (Ed.), *The Routledge companion to alternative and community media* (pp. 1–18). Routledge.

Atton, C., & Hamilton, J. F. (2008). *Alternative journalism*. Sage.

Berrigan, F. J. (1979). Community communications: The role of community media in development. Reports and Papers on mass communication. *UNESCO*. https://unesdoc.unesco.org/ark:/48223/pf0000044035

Biswal, P. K. (2018, August 29). Rural journalism in a shambles. The Statesman. https://www.thestatesman.com/opinion/rural-journalism-shambles-1502712969.html

Bosch, T. (2008). Theorizing citizen's media: A rhizomatic approach. In D. Kidd, C. Rodriguez, & L. Stein (Eds.), *Making our media: Global initiatives towards a democratic public sphere* (pp. 71–89). Hampton Press.

Bowman, S., & Willis, C. (2003). "We Media: How audiences are shaping the future of news & information." https://ict4peace.org/wp-content/uploads/2007/05/we_media.pdf

Bruns, A. (2010). From reader to writer; Citizen journalism as news produsage. In J. Hunsinger, L. Klastrup, & M. Allen (Eds.), *International handbook of internet research* (pp. 119–134). Springer.

Bruns, A. (2015). Working the story: News curation in social media as a second wave of citizen journalism. In C. Atton (Ed.), *The Routledge companion to alternative and community media* (pp. 379–388). Routledge.

Bruns, A. (2016). 'Random acts of journalism' redux: News and social media. In J. L. Jensen, M. Mortensen, & J. Ørmen (Eds.), *News across media*. Production, distribution and consumption (pp. 32–47). Routledge.

Carpenter, S. (2008). How online citizen journalism publications and online newspapers utilize the objectivity standard and rely on external sources. *Journalism & Mass Communication Quarterly*, *85*(3), 531–548.

Carpenter, S. (2009). An examination of news quality and the extent to which U.S. online newspaper and online citizen journalism publications adhere to it. In J. Rosenberry & B. St. John III (Eds.), *Public journalism 2.0: The promise and reality of a citizen-engaged press*. Routledge.

Carpenter, S. (2019). Citizen journalism. *Oxford Research Encyclopedia*. doi: 10.1093/acrefore/9780190228613.013.786

Carroll, W. K., & Hackett, R. A. (2006). Democratic media activism through the lens of social movement theory. *Media, Culture & Society*, *28*(1), 83–104.

Castells, M. (2009). *Communication power*. Oxford University Press.

Chadha, K., & Steiner, L. (2015). The potential and limitations of citizen journalism initiatives. The case of India's CGNet Swara. *Journalism Studies*, *16*(5), 706–718.

Corsa, S. (2014). Media for the masses: The usage patterns and social consequences of a mobile-phone based citizen journalism platform in Madhya Pradesh. https://digitalcollections.sit.edu/isp_collection/1952/

Philip, S., & Dutta, D.(2022). Beyond the pandemic: The struggles of Chhattisgarh's Adivasis. India Development Review. https://idronline.org/article/social-justice/beyond-the-pandemic-the-struggles-of-chhattisgarhs-adivasis/

Ekström, M., & Östman, J. (2015). Information, interaction, and creative production: The effects of three forms of internet use on youth democratic engagement. *Communication Research*, *42*(6). https://journals.sagepub.com/doi/10.1177/0093650213476295

ET Bureau (2022, July 28). Rural India is driving internet adoption, survey finds. *Economic Times*. https://economictimes.indiatimes.com/tech/technology/rural-india-is-driving-internet-adoption-survey-finds/articleshow/93186625.cms?from=mdr

exchange4media Staff (2007, November 17). *e4m.com* https://www.exchange4media.com/media-tv-news/cnn-ibn-to-celebrate-citizen-activism-with-the-citizen-journalist-showbe-the-change-28616.html

Fforde, S. (2019). Alternative journalism around the world. In C. Atton (Ed.), *The Routledge companion to alternative and community media* (pp. 291–300). Routledge.

Friedland, L., & Rojas, H. Public Sphere Project (n.d.). http://www.publicsphereproject.org/node/290

Freire, P. (1970). *Pedagogy of the oppressed*. Continuum.

GramVaani.org (2019). https://gramvaani.org/the-mobilevaani-manifesto/

Gram Vaani.org (n.d.). Girls can now access locked toilet. *Gram Vaani*. https://gramvaani.org/collective-action-girls-can-now-access-the-school-toilet-which-was-kept-locked/

Hackett, R., & Carroll, W. (2006). *Remaking media: The struggle to democratic public communication*. Routledge.

Harcup, T. (2019). Alternative journalism. In J. F. Nussbaum (Ed.), *Oxford Research Encyclopedia of Communication*. Oxford University Press. https://oxfordre.com/communication/display/10.1093/acrefore/9780190228613.001.0001/acrefore-9780190228613-e-780?d=%2F10.1093%2Facrefore%2F9780190228613.001.0001%2Facrefore-9780190228613-e-780&p=emailAWzyKly00HHgU

Hoffman, J. (2006, December 10). Sousveillance. *New York Times*. https://www.nytimes.com/2006/12/10/magazine/10section3b.t-3.html

Howley, K. (2005). *Community media: People, places, and communication technologies*. Cambridge University Press.

Inamdar, S. (2018). *CGNet Swara: Journalism and governance in rural India*. Masters thesis. https://openrepository.aut.ac.nz/items/e66b71a1-1fcb-4ff4-b196-78561687d527

Kaufhold, K., Valenzuala, S., & Gil de Zuniga, H. (2010). Citizen journalism and democracy: How user-generated news use relates to political knowledge and participation. *Journalism and Mass Communication Quarterly, 87* (3–4). doi: 10.1177/107769901008700305

Kaushik, A., & Suchiang, A. (2022). Introduction. In A. Kaushik, & A. Suchiang (Eds.), *Narratives and new voices from India. Cases for community development and social change* (pp. 1–10). Springer.

Kern, T., & Nam, S. (2009). The making of a social movement: Citizen journalism in South Korea. *Current Sociology, 57*(5). doi: 10.1177/0011392109337649

Kruks-Wisner, G. (2022). Social brokerage: Accountability and the social life of information. *Comparative Political Studies, 56*(14), 2382–2415.

Marathe, M., O'Neill, J., Pain, P., & Thies, W. (2015). Revisiting *CGNet Swara* and its impact in rural India. *Proceedings of the 2015 International Conference on Information and Communication Technologies and Development (ICTD)*.

Mehta, D. (2021, December 6). A guide to using the WhatsApp Business API for audience engagement. Journalist Support Committee. https://www.journalistsupport.net/article.php?id=377450

Melkote, S. R., & Steeves, H. L. (2001). *Communication for development in the third world: Theory and practice for empowerment*. Sage.

Moitra, A., Das, V., Gram Vaani team, Kumar, A. & Seth, A. (2016). Design lessons from creating a mobile-based community media platform in India. *Proceedings of the 2016 International Conference on Information and Communication Technologies and Development (ICTD)*.

Mudgal, V. (2011). Rural coverage in the Hindi and English dailies. *Economic & Political Weekly, 46*(35), 92–97.

Mudliar, P., & Donner, J. (2015). Experiencing interactive voice response (IVR) as a participatory medium: The case of *CGNet Swara* in India. *Mobile Media and Communication, 3*(3), 366–382.

Mudliar, P., Donner, J., & Thies, W. (2012). Emergent practices around *CGNet Swara*: A voice forum for citizen journalism in rural India. *Proceedings of the 2012 International Conference on Information and Communication Technologies and Development (ICTD)*.

Murthy, C. H. S. N. (2015). Issues of rural development in mainstream journalism: Exploring new strategies for media intervention. *Journal of Global Communication, 8*, 23–35.

Mutsvairo, B., & Salgado, S. (2022). Is citizen journalism dead? An examination of recent developments in the field. *Journalism, 2*(23). https://doi.org/10.1177/1464884920968440

Nah, S., Namkoong, K., Record, R., & Van Stee, S. (2017). Citizen journalism practice increases civic participation. *Newspaper Research Journal, 38*(1), 62–78.

Nah, S., & Yamamoto, M. (2020). Citizen journalism, political discussion, and civic participation: Testing a moderating role of media credibility and collective efficacy. *International Journal of Communication, 14*, 5177–5198.

Nath, P. J. (2015, December). The fifth pillar. *The Hindu.* https://www.thehindu.com/ social/citizen-journalists-relayed-asithappened-news-that-was-taken-forward-by-media/article7992088.ece

Ninan, S. (2007). Headlines from the heartland: Reinventing the Hindi public sphere. SagePublications.

Noor, R. (2013). Citizen journalism and cultural migration of media: A case study of *Cj. IBNLive. Trends in Information Management, 9*(1), 54–67.

Pain, P. (2018). Ear to the ground or useless entities? Citizen journalism and mainstream media in India. *Communication Research and Practice, 4*(4), 396–411.

Pain, P., Khalid, M. Z., & Ahmed, A. (2022). "CGNet Swara encourages us to participate and bring about change": Analyzing the role of media and development. In A. Kaushik, & A. Suchiang (Eds.), *Narratives and new voices from India. Cases for community development and social change* (pp. 43–57). Springer.

Pajnik, M. (2019). Changing citizenship, practicing (alternative) politics. In C. Atton (Ed.), *The Routledge companion to alternative and community media* (pp.113–122). Routledge.

Quintero, C.P., Hincapie, C.E.R., & Rodriguez, C. (2019). Cameras and stories to disarm wars. Performative communication in alternative media. In C. Atton (ed.). The Routledge Companion to Alternative and Community Media (pp. 123–133). Routledge.

Rai, R. (2011, July 8). NREGA: Worked for 100 days not even paid for a day. *CG Net Swara.org.* http://www.cgnetswara.org/index.php?id=276

Rheingold, H. (1993). *The virtual community: Homesteading on the electronic frontier.* MIT Press.

Roberts, J. (2019). Citizen journalism. In R. Hobbs and P. Mihalidis (Eds.), *The international encyclopedia of media literacy.* John Wiley & Sons, Inc. **doi:** 10.1002/9781118978238.iem10027

Roberts, J., & Steiner, L. (2012). The ethics of citizen journalism. In D. Heider, & A. Massanari (Eds.), *Digital ethics: Research & practice* (pp. 80–98). Peter Lang.

Rodriguez, C. (2001). *Fissures in the mediascape. An international study of citizens' media.* Hampton Press.

Rutigliano, L. W. (2008). *Covering the unknown city: Citizen journalism and marginalized communities.* Unpublished dissertation, The University of Texas at Austin

Saha, A. (2012). Cell phones as tool for democracy: The example of CGNet Swara. *Economic & Political Weekly, 14*, 23–26.

Singer, J., Hermida, A., Domingo, D., Heinonen, A., Paulussen, S., Quandt, T., Reich, Z., & Vujnovic, M. (2011). *Participatory journalism: Guarding open gates at online newspapers.* Wiley Blackwell.

Smith, R. (2014, June 18). Shubhranshu Choudhary: Giving a voice to a ravaged, neglected region. *National Geographic.* https://www.nationalgeographic.com/ culture/article/140617-shubhranshu-choudhary-india-maoists-citizen-journalism

Sonwalkar, P. (2009). Citizen journalism in India: The politics of recognition. In S. Allan, & E. Thorsen (Eds.), *Citizen journalism: Global perspectives* (pp. 75–84). Peter Lang.

Thomas, P. (2012). News makers in the era of citizen journalism: The view from India. In J. Clarke, & M. Bromley (Eds.), *International news in the digital age: East-West perceptions of a new world* (pp. 149–168). Routledge.

Thussu, D. K. (2007). *News as entertainment–The rise of global infotainment.* Sage. Video Volunteers.org.https://www.videovolunteers.org/about/video-volunteers-background-what-is-community-media/

Video Volunteers (n.d.). About Us. LinkedIn.com. https://www.linkedin.com/company/video-volunteers

Video Volunteers.org (2023). Impact. https://www.videovolunteers.org/category/videos/impact-indiaunheard/

5 Khabar Lahariya

Women-Produced Digital Journalism in Rural India

People would not think of me as a journalist—how can women become journalists? That's not their job. They should be home, taking care of children, doing what the man of the house asks them to do. So initially people would chase us out, and not give us information. Being a Dalit and a woman journalist, that was an even greater crime.

—Kavita Davi (Murti, 2020)

We were not trained in using computers. We were not trained in journalism… We went where governments, mainstream media, and politicians had never gone before. We listened to people's stories. And we went back again and again. It took us years to be accepted… Change did not happen overnight, of course, ours has been a two decade-long journey. But we have believed and stuck to our first principles. Rural marginalized women write on issues that matter to us and our communities.

—Meera Jatav (GIJN Staff, 2022)

Khabar Lahariya: Origins, History and Emergence as Digital News Outlet

These are excerpts from recent interviews with two founding members of *Khabar Lahariya* (meaning News Wave in the local dialect of the region where it was founded), a digital news organization focusing on rural issues. Managed by a 40-person team made up entirely of women—many of whom, including its leadership, are drawn from marginalized groups—Khabar Lahariya's news room is actively engaged in reporting from the hinterlands of northern and central India.

But unlike mainstream outlets whose reporting choices are largely governed by what Allern (2002) identified as "commercial news values," such as perceived competition, type of audience and corporate financial objectives (also clearly manifest in the Indian context), the *Khabar Lahariya* collective instead defines itself as engaging in "rural journalism that follows the everyday stories of everyday people in areas that are completely out of the spotlight of media attention" (*Khabar Lahariya, LinkedIn.com*). As a reporter for the outlet put it, "news is not just the headlines of big newspapers but a handpump which is broken in a village, which is 50 kilometers away from the district

DOI: 10.4324/9781003244202-5

headquarters... that's equally important news" (Splice Media, 2020). While one of its co-founders said:

> We write about the condition of roads and sewers. We write about the lack of access to electricity, water, and work. You might think these are very ordinary things to write about, but for us this is what makes the difference between whether villages get roads or not, whether Dalit neighborhoods are cleaned or not, whether hand pumps are fixed or not, in order for women to fulfill their family's water requirements. We write about the unwaged, unseen labor of women who work in informal economies... We write about the Dalit woman whose complaint will not be taken up by the police because the perpetrator is a powerful, upper-caste male.
>
> (GIJN Staff, 2022)

Put differently, *Khabar Lahariya* thus engages in the production of what Franklin and Murphy (1991) have referred to as "the production of revelatory news" or topics that directly impact the lives of working people in their communities (p. 106). In other words, both what the organization covers "bypassing the event-driven routines of mainstream news practices" (Atton, 2010, p. 173) and the manner in which it approaches news production is not only different but arguably also more transparent than legacy media where journalists as Hall (1973) has argued, "speak of 'the news' as if events select themselves" (p. 181). The organization also differentiates itself from mainstream news entities in the way that it explicitly identifies itself as a feminist news organization whose news reports "question structures of power and inequity in the personal sphere of the family, as well as in the public realm" (Schirn Mag, 2022 As one of its founders explained, "We're sort of like a local watchdog with a feminist lens" (Schirn Mag, 2022).

Although now a digital-only news outlet, *Khabar Lahariya* (see Figure 5.1) launched in 2002 in the Chitrakoot district of the Bundelkhand region that stretches across parts of the northern state of Uttar Pradesh and the central state of Madhya Pradesh. Initially, the publication started as a fortnightly, print newspaper that carried articles—written in the local Bundeli dialect as well as Hindi—and which "in its own unique style covered everything from local to global news" (Naqvi, 2007, p. 13). The publication, which was entirely reported, produced and distributed by a team of seven local women, emerged out of the *Mahila Dakiya* (translated as post-woman, in a nod to its role in delivering news), a handwritten broadsheet "newspaper" that had been produced in the 1990s by participants in the *Mahila Samakhya* program. Recognized as "a major achievement of the Indian feminist movement," this government-funded initiative sought to empower women from marginalized low-caste and tribal communities through development and literacy-related activities (Das, 2020).

Figure 5.1 Screenshot from *Khabar Lahariya* website showing the impact of fog on crops.

The underlying impetus for the establishment of *Khabar Lahariya*'s predecessor *Mahila Dakiya*, came about as the women involved in the government program sought mechanisms to communicate with other women in the local region. Thus, whereas generally rising literacy stimulates a demand for news, here it was women's "entry into the public sphere and their increased public participation, which created the need for a newspaper" (Naqvi, 2007, p. 44). Established in 1993—with the help of a Delhi-based gender education NGO *Nirantar* that was assisting with the implementation of the *Mahila Samakhya* program—the publication was defined, from the outset, by the active participation of its readers in the processes of news production. Spivak (1988) has pointed out that colonialism and indigenous patriarchal structures in India engendered a state of "epistemic violence" that disregarded women's situated knowledge while also denying them access to education and expression. And although the colonial state disappeared with the achievement of independence in 1947, women, especially those in conservative rural contexts, continued to lack the ability to speak for themselves or indeed speak at all. *The Mahila Dakiya* project constituted an attempt to reverse this situation by giving women "control over the written word," and in so doing, "giving them control over construction and representation of their own reality" (Naqvi, 2007, p. 46).

The emphasis on involving women—who ranged from being newly literate to having a primary school education—was a deliberate act aimed at not only enabling women to produce accessible reading material focused on local content but also undermining caste and gender hierarchies whose deep-rooted structures had traditionally prevented women in the region from engaging in public-facing activities. Following principles of inclusion and collaboration that defined *Nirantar's* ethos as a feminist organization, the production of the paper was put together during workshops where participants had the opportunity to engage in debate and contestation. Indeed, it was discussions among the women that determined both format and the content covered by the publication.

Similarly, it was the women who decided that the publication should be a single broadsheet with illustrations and a large font size that could be pasted onto a wall and read in a group setting, while also determining that in addition to a combination of some local and national news, the news agenda should primarily focus on women's personal experiences, news related to health, politics, government programs and schemes, all the while centering questions of development from the women's perspective (*Nirantar* Workshop Report quoted in Naqvi, 2007). In its news values, the paper thus reflected a fairly sophisticated understanding of the interests of potential readers (i.e. neo or semi-literate rural women). Moreover, as such, it not only represented a form of feminist journalism in which gender served as a defining lens in determining the newsworthiness of content but also constituted a challenge to the manner in which traditional news reporting is "structurally circumscribed by patterns of ownership in media industries and influenced by 'news values,' 'hierarchies of credibility,' 'journalistic routines' and dominant cultural assumptions" (Kitzinger, 1998, p. 186).

In 1995, *Mahila Dakiya* transformed itself from being a program-sponsored publication into the country's first community newspaper (Das, 2020). And though the general format and content remained consistent with its past avatar, this shift nevertheless engendered an enhanced sense of the need for "responsibility" and accountability with regard to what was published (Naqvi, 2007). As a 1995 *Nirantar* report put it, "since the readers were all local residents, errors of fact or interpretation were easily spotted. This close relationship with readers was both a blessing and a peril of civic journalism…in some ways this meant that MD had to adhere to higher standards of accuracy than most mainstream papers." (*Nirantar* Meeting Report, quoted in Naqvi,

2007). In other words, its reporting followed the pattern of many alternative journalism outlets that, according to Atton (2010), parallel mainstream news organizations in "their pursuit of accuracy," even as they "eschew some of the other norms and conventions of the latter" (p. 174). But despite receiving a national journalism award in 1996–1997, the paper struggled due to external competition from "professional" regional Hindi-language newspapers that were expanding significantly into rural areas during the 1980s and 1990s "as a result of the increased literacy, improved communication and rising rural incomes, as well as aggressive marketing strategies adopted by publishers" (Ninan, 2007, p. 113). The publication also had internal issues such as the inability to price appropriately, lack of advertising as well as a reliable distribution mechanism (Naqvi, 2007). Eventually, in the year 2000, *Mahila Dakiya* ceased to operate.

In 2002, some of the women who had been involved with the paper decided to launch their own publication in the form of *Khabar Lahariya*. This new publication was envisioned as a "real rural newspaper," one that offered a comprehensive range of coverage that went beyond gender concerns and development issues to encompass more local politics and news reporting, even as it retained the feminist perspective that had defined its predecessor, *Mahila Dakiya* (Naqvi, 2007, p. 104). Commenting on the group's motivation for establishing the paper, one of its founders said that their primary goal was to address a "gap" in the region which lacked "an independent paper that was not influenced by corporate or political agendas," while simultaneously finding ways to give space to "women voices" and tell "stories from their points of view" (Doshi, 2016). As a *Khabar Lahariya* co-founder referring to the rural coverage said, "local stories from the rural heartlands of India didn't go beyond udghatan (inauguration), durghatna (accident) and hatya (murder) (Naqvi, 2007). Furthermore, patterns of representation were controlled by rural reporters for mainstream Hindi newspapers (who were mostly stringers from small towns), so that rural citizens were portrayed as "the other, different, non-literate and therefore non-intelligent" (Naqvi, 2007, p. 17). In other words, "the rural-urban power hierarchy remained essentially untouched," with the result that mainstream news accounts of rural life were dominated by images of "helpless victimhood," with rural citizens demonstrating little sense of agency (Naqvi, 2007, p. 17).

Khabar Lahariya with its commitment to the idea of creating "a gender sensitive, caste sensitive paper," containing hyperlocal news aimed at readers in remote rural areas, thus positioned itself, albeit implicitly, as an alternative to commercial Hindi newspapers offered little coverage of local or gender related issues except on rare occasions when they reported on some sensational or gruesome event. In doing so, the paper not only challenged the hegemony of mainstream media outlets—which in India are almost exclusively controlled and regulated by upper caste men (Tomar, 2014)—but also called into question a variety of societal constraints. Explaining the significance of her involvement with the paper, one of the reporters said "I come from a village where women still live behind the purdah," referring to the tradition of keeping women confined within domestic spaces. "When I started working, it was the first time I had ever left my house alone" (Doshi, 2016).

At the same time however, unlike its predecessor *Mahila Dakiya* which was fundamentally associated with improving female literacy, the new paper "aspired to mainstream accountability and a more mainstream look" (Naqvi, 2007, p. 107). Consequently, it embarked on the introduction of greater professionalization in terms of organization, training, journalistic practices and range of coverage. For instance, the newsroom hired paid workers who were divided into groups focusing on news gathering, distribution and management. Furthermore, the paper's reporters were trained in different aspects of journalism such as reporting techniques, verification and writing as well as photography. Eventually, the paper which had originated as a handwritten product (Sinha, & Malik, 2022) evolved into an eight-page publication with seven sections (such as Women's Issues, Development, Letters and Editorials) and began to be produced via desktop publishing (personal communication, *Khabar Lahariya* team member, 2023). In keeping with the push toward greater professionalization, *Khabar Lahariya* was also formally registered as a newspaper in 2005. And for the next decade, the all-women journalist team wrote, edited, produced, distributed and marketed the newspaper in the villages and towns of the Bundelkhand region in Uttar Pradesh.

On February 13, 2013, the paper went online. As Poorvi Bhargava, an editorial coordinator for the paper at the time, put it:

It's not a question of 'why' rather it is why we didn't do it sooner…we always wanted to take our story online… it's a misconception that rural areas are unaware of internet. Web is making big inroads, thanks to smartphones. But, most sites either do not carry rural news or carry it in a language alien to these people. That is where the *Khabar Lahariya* website comes in …

(Roy, n.d.)

In its online form, the paper closely resembled its physical counterpart in that its website was designed with new or recently literate readers in mind. The layout was simple and the font size, just like the printed newspaper, was made larger than usual to make it easy to read. It was also the only news website where content was available in local dialects such as Bundeli, Bajjka and Avadhi, thereby offering a challenge to the linguistic dominance of mainstream Hindi papers (Tomar, 2014).

Moreover, like its print version, digital *Khabar Lahariya* was similarly produced by a cadre of rural women reporters supported by urban NGO members and media practitioners. Drawn in significant numbers from rural Dalit, Muslim and tribal Kol communities, that were among some of the most oppressed groups in the region, these women were trained in the basics of internet use (learning how to browse the web and send and receive emails) as well as multimedia journalism such as using cell phones to take photos and record video stories. And while this might have been considered mundane in more urban contexts, this was a major step for rural women who not only lacked access to phones or computers but tended, in the words of one of *Khabar Lahariya*'s founders, to view devices "with a fear in their mind" that "things would break" if they used them (Roy, n.d.). Such training not only enhanced their reporting abilities but also acted as a source of personal transformation. As a young woman describing the impact of learning the basics of how to report using digital technology expressed it:

> We learnt so many things, about the internet, about videography, photography. I feel like something has opened up inside, I'm feeling very free, like my way of thinking has expanded so much.
>
> (Roy, n.d.)

While another said:

> I feel that my stories are deeper because I can use Google to do more research… And I can use a selfie stick, and a smartphone and connect with other people. I feel professional…
>
> (Roy, n.d.)

With the rapid, close to a 100%, increase in internet penetration combined with growing smart phone access in rural India, by late 2015, *Khabar Lahariya* pivoted to what could be termed a digital first strategy to reach both existing and potential audiences. In fact, video emerged as the primary medium for the outlet's reporting and its reporters began filing video reports and instant updates on WhatsApp and Facebook where the outlet already had a presence (personal communication, *Khabar Lahariya* team member, 2023). Underscoring the importance of this shift, a senior reporter with the publication said:

> Using video increased our prestige…It is easy to work with, and it shows people that we are on the ground and reporting facts, that we're not just making things up.
>
> (Doshi, 2016)

As in the case of mainstream news organizations, in addition to changes in technology use, the digital first strategy also resulted in the adoption of new journalistic practices that reflected the imperatives of online journalism, especially its emphasis on speed and immediacy. Thus, whereas the paper's original website had contained stories that had already appeared in its print edition—in a variation of the shovelware common among early online news organizations which tended to use their websites to simply "recycle their printed copy in a new channel" (Dimitrova & Neznanski, 2006, p. 248), *Khabar Lahariya* now began to first publish every story online on platforms, including Facebook, various WhatsApp groups, as well as on its website, while its weekly print edition came to be comprised of stories drawn from its digital output. Commenting on this shift, one of the outlet's leaders said that *Khabar Lahariya* had turned "the system on its head," going as it did from "a weekly print paper to publishing videos and photos on a daily basis on Face-book, WhatsApp and the website" (Dixit, 2016).

In addition to changing the manner in which they produced news, *Khabar Lahariya,* in line with professional digital news outlets, also had to develop a mechanism that could support a team of paid reporters. This resulted in the formation of *Chambal Media*, a self-defined "digital media social enterprise," whose goal was to create a financially sustainable model "to distribute and market content produced by and relevant for rural audiences online" (Dixit, 2016). Thus, while *Khabar Lahariya* was initially established as a not-for-profit enterprise in association with the NGO *Nirantar*, *Chambal Media* was set up as a commercial umbrella organization that sought to market the out-let's work and services. It did so by providing syndicated content and acting as a news agency for other media, offering content to NGOs and foundations working on rural issues as well as offering rural consumer insights into brands and using the funds generated to support the news operations of *Khabar Lahariya* (Park, 2020).

In 2016, the outlet went entirely digital, launching social media pages, including a Twitter handle, a YouTube Channel, and its own mobile app (Sinha, 2022). In part, this decision stemmed from continuing problems of newspaper distribution in remote areas but it was also driven by the fact that the use of smart phones to access news on social media platforms was becoming increas-ingly commonplace in rural India. According to editor in chief, Kavita Devi, anxious to take advantage of this development, the paper decided to entirely pivot away from print to digital, with the aim of reaching "more people than just the educated men who live in well-connected villages by the highway" (Agarwal, 2017). In a similar vein, Disha Mullick, a co-founder of *Chambal Media*, made the point that the transition to a digital-only publication not only enabled the outlet to overcome its struggles with distribution but social media enabled *Khabar Lahariya* to "spread our news because so many young people accessed the internet through their smartphones" (Ananya, 2016). Not surpris-ingly, this also impacted the outlet's audience composition, shifting it away from older men to a younger demographic made up of individuals between 18-35 years of age. This group, moreover, included a significant number of women readers, whose numbers increased by 35% immediately following the shift to digital platforms (Ananya, 2016).

Since then, the outlet has expanded its footprint from the Bundelkhand area (where it was originally launched) into other districts of Uttar Pradesh as well as into neighboring states in central and eastern India. Indeed, according to the organization, *Khabar Lahariya* reaches up to "10 million people every month through multiple digital platforms. It has a network of 30 local women reporters across 25-30 districts, who run a hyperlocal, video-first news channel, broadcasting news primarily to audiences in remote areas of Uttar Pradesh, Madhya Pradesh and Bihar" (Chambal Media, n.d.), producing about 200 stories every month. *Khabar Lahariya* has an especially significant presence on WhatsApp groups and YouTube where it has more than 150 million views and over 540,000 subscribers (Chambal Media, n.d.). Commenting on these developments, Kavita Devi stated that:

> Technology that is easily accessible to people at the bottom of the pyramid is most effective. In the last two years, YouTube and WhatsApp have revolutionized how people access and share news and they have changed the way our newsroom works in a very positive way. YouTube has helped *Khabar Lahariya* to jump the literacy barriers. We've been able to reach many more women and non-literate people in villages through the platform.
> (Luepker, 2019)

In the *Khabar Lahariya* distribution model, news stories are first published on YouTube, then on the website and subsequently on multiple social media platforms such as X and Instagram where *Khabar Lahariya* maintains a presence. *Khabar Lahariya* has also relaunched its prior youth-oriented "long reads" subscription service Sound, Fury and 4G (SFG4) in the form of a subscription-based English-language product called *KL Hatke*.[1] This product adapts hyperlocal news stories by contextualizing them in relation to larger issues such as labor rights, climate change and women's rights for urban and international readers who have emerged as a major secondary audience for its content (personal communication with *Khabar Lahariya* team member, 2023).

Khabar Lahariya: A Feminist Newsroom at Work

While *Khabar Lahariya* has demonstrated considerable innovation in its journalistic evolution, notably its embrace of digital technologies and social media platforms, arguably what makes it demonstrably different from both mainstream and alternative digital news outlets in India is its all women newsroom, characterized by a horizontal and collaborative work culture. Historically, women journalists have had a limited presence in Indian newsrooms and those who belong to marginalized communities have been virtually absent. This makeup of mainstream newsrooms has not changed despite the massive expansion of the media sector that began in the 1990s. Indeed, a 2015 study of gender representation in Indian media found that despite entering the profession in significant numbers, women continue to be a minority in Indian journalism, being concentrated in the lower and middle rungs of the profession (International Federation of Journalists). More recently, data compiled by the media watchdog group *Newslaundry* in conjunction with the United Nations, came to similarly discouraging conclusions. Their analysis found that except for independent digital media outlets where women made up about one-third of the editorial staff, gender representation in mainstream media continues to be "mostly tokenistic," and even when women were employed, there was generally "little diversity across caste, religious and ethnic background" (*Newslaundry*, 2022).

Not surprisingly, the study also found that leadership positions in India's newsrooms were dominated by men and that women were hampered by sexism, sexual harassment as well as gender-based appraisal and promotion procedures that tended to favor men (*Newslaundry*, 2022). In contrast, the *Khabar Lahariya* newsroom, in addition to being wholly staffed by women, since its inception, has been constructed along egalitarian lines (personal communication, *Khabar Lahariya* team member, 2023). While this involved a process of trial and error as KL sought to "reach a compromise between a perfect collective and absolute hierarchy" (Naqvi, 2007, p. 110), the outlet gradually developed a team-based structure. In this organizational structure, women were assigned to different types of roles ranging from stringers to reporter, although "these designations" were somewhat "misleading" because all the women undertook other tasks, with the result that "power was shared on many fronts," as the paper was put together during fortnightly residential production workshops (Naqvi, 2007, p. 122). Over time this team-based model has acquired a more dispersed structure. At present, the publication relies on a New Delhi-based team of eight or nine women who are responsible for editing and publishing news stories, and field reporters who operate in the districts that *Khabar Lahariya* covers. The women in the field cover all beats and are fairly autonomous in their everyday work, making decisions on reporting while being connected to the editorial operations of *Khabar Lahariya* (through WhatsApp and Gmail) for feedback and editing.

This type of collective, non-hierarchical approach—that according to Atton (2010), often defines alternative journalism projects—emerged out of *Nirantar*'s feminist ideals and its efforts to subvert the power differential that often exists between urban NGOs and the rural communities with whom they work. The result has been a collective-style newsroom where even as rural women acquire journalistic skills, they also educate others—including their NGO sponsors—about rural issues based on their situated knowledge. Thus, news production occurs in an interactive and decentralized manner, with a collaborative work culture that presents a stark contrast to what Tomar (2014) calls the "lobbying culture" of mainstream newsroom, which appears *"as a neutral 'professional journalism ethos,'"* while being *"for all practical and ideological purposes, organized around a man-as-norm and women-as-interloper structure,"* (Byerly & Ross, 2006, p. 79). In other words, it militates against the gendered substructures "embedded in newsroom practices, e.g. male preferences setting the agenda for news selection; the typical male/female division of labor in the beat allocation," (de Bruin, 2014, p. 52) that result in the marginalization of women in newsroom hierarchies.

Khabar Lahariya also stands apart from mainstream news organizations in terms of the intentionally intersectional composition of its newsroom—a choice that has significant implications for the news that the outlet produces. As in the case of its non-hierarchical approach to newsroom organization, the emphasis on intersectionality dates back to the origins *of Mahila Dakiya* and its efforts to engage women from marginalized communities. As a concept, intersectionality was developed by legal scholar Kimberlé Crenshaw (1989) who employed it to refer to the double discrimination of racism and sexism faced by Black women. Critiquing what she deemed to be the "single-axis framework that is dominant in antidiscrimination law… feminist theory and anti-racist politics," (p. 149) Crenshaw suggested that the notion of intersectionality constituted "a metaphor for understanding the ways that multiple forms of inequality or disadvantage sometimes compound themselves and create obstacles that often are not understood among conventional ways of thinking" (p. 149). In the Indian context, intersectionality offers a powerful lens to understand the experiences of women who belong to Dalit and tribal communities that are located squarely at the bottom of India's social order and consequently experience interlocking systems of social and economic exclusion. Indeed, Dalit feminists have long asserted that the:

Interventionist approaches typified by mainstream Indian feminism fails to address issues concerning Dalit women because mainstream Indian feminisms tend to see caste and gender as two separate and mutually exclusive categories. Dalit feminism, on the other hand, sees caste and gender as two interrelated structures that actively and simultaneously contribute to the structural oppression of Dalit women, and it argues that mainstream Indian feminism often suppresses socio-cultural differences such as in caste identity, in order to magnify particular issues and impose universality as "women."

(Pan, 2023, p. 6)

More specifically, according to Dalit feminists, the very positionality of Dalit women in the Indian social order subjects them to different types of structural forces that "intersect" or work in concert against them. As they put it:

We are concerned that Dalit women in India suffer from three oppressions: gender, as a result of patriarchy; class, being from the poorest and most marginalized communities; and caste, coming from the lowest caste, the "untouchables."

(National Federation of Dalit Women, 2009)

And it is such Dalit women (along with a handful of Muslim women) who make up a significant number of *Khabar Lahariya*'s staff. Discussing the outlet's approach to creating a newsroom whose members experienced overlapping or intersectional forms of structural discrimination, *Chambal Media* co-founder Disha Mullick said that this decision was underpinned by a feminist understanding of the marginalization experienced by low caste women (in society as well as news media coverage) and a concomitant desire to redress this situation. Elaborating on this, she said:

> In the Indian context and in *Khabar Lahariya*'s context, caste has been crucial... the media like other domains of knowledge, like the university systems or other knowledge systems are controlled by upper-castes. In India, the caste system has meant that you're born into certain kinds of roles and livelihoods generationally and over centuries. And those at the top of the caste hierarchy are also those who have access to knowledge - the creation of it and the consumption of it. And traditionally, Dalits who are outside of the caste system or are at the lowest fringes of the caste system...and Dalit women are even more so... the idea for *Khabar Lahariya* was two-fold. It was to be able to have a voice in the media which was not the voice that we hear generally - And the other thing was to have stories in mainstream media which were not being covered by mainstream media.
> (Splice Media, 2020)

However, the decision to staff the newsroom with women at the bottom of the social hierarchy was not merely an idealistic one. As Gerlis (2008) points out, a key aim of alternative journalism is to "turn journalism from a lecture into a conversation" by encouraging consumers of news to become creators of news" arguably for their ability to provide unique insights into their own lifeworlds—a point underscored by the outlet's editor in chief, Kavita Devi. The only Dalit member of the Editor's Guild of India, Devi has argued that despite limited education, women from low caste/otherwise marginalized communities bring an important perspective to *Khabar Lahariya*. According to her:

> We'd decided to work with Dalit, Adivasi, Muslim—basically women from the margins. A lot of these women had only primary school educations. Some couldn't write anything beyond their own name. A lot of women we work with began studying only after they started working with us. But, the thing is, while we interviewed these women, they answered questions about the areas they lived in with ease and expertise. This made me think—these women aren't literate or educated, but they're extremely well versed with the societal norms, community, general affairs, and geography of the regions they're from. What else do you need from a good reporter?
> (Splice Media, 2020)

This decision was not uncontroversial. As Naqvi (2007) writes, whereas the adoption of a feminist perspective or what a team member referred to as the "nariwadi nazariya," (*Khabar Lahariya* team member, personal communication, 2023) was easily accepted, not only did it take some effort before the Dalit women in the newsroom "became more self-aware" regarding their "caste-based social location" but also initially produced some resistance from non-Dalit women who "were threatened by the *Khabar Lahariya*'s emerging Dalit identity and saw it as exclusionary" (p. 127). After considerable internal debate, including discussions, about the intersectional oppression experienced by Dalit women, the outlet's journalists not only "became increasingly comfortable with a Dalit political location" but also actively sought out stories focusing on Dalits (Naqvi, 2007, p. 128).

But though this intersectional approach characterizes the *Khabar Lahariya* newsroom, the latter does not define itself exclusively as a Dalit paper or a women's paper, but rather as a hyperlocal rural outlet, albeit one that is informed by an awareness of both gender and caste/class concerns. In this regard, co-founder Kavita Devi observed that although initially people had assumed that an all-women newsroom would only focus on "soft" or so-called "women's issues," *Khabar Lahariya* actually took a broader approach. In this context, she said:

We started covering rural news on the ground-level, going to remote villages where mainstream media wouldn't even think of going. Those remote places included Adivasi (tribal) communities, jungle areas, places where media couldn't reach, areas occupied by dacoits...We did exposes of local level corruption by government officials...We developed a distinct kind of brand of story-telling...women's stories, political stories, crime stories, anything that has local relevance, with stakeholders and respondents who are from communities whose voices often don't reach the mainstream media headlines.

(Splice Media, 2020)

This approach is apparent in *Khabar Lahariya*'s coverage that covers a range of local issues. For instance, the paper's website has specific sections devoted exclusively to development, crimes against women, local and national politics with a particular focus on elections titled at various levels, as well as a feature section with in-depth reporting on a range of the socio-economic and cultural concerns of rural communities, many of them with a particular focus on their implications for lower castes and women, identities that often define the reporters as well. Not surprisingly, this reprises inevitable questions about the place of advocacy and activism in their work. While the women do not claim to adhere to the "regime of objectivity," (Hackett & Carroll, 2006) in the way that so-called "mainstream organizations do," they certainly see their work as "reporting" and not "advocacy" or campaigning for an issue. Consequently, according to *Khabar Lahariya* co-founder Kavita Devi, the main focus of reporters is on "bringing a story into the public domain," and relying on their sustained, "rigorous" reporting to have an impact on the resolution of issues, rather than advocating for a particular cause or outcome.

On an everyday basis, *Khabar Lahariya* reporters produce multimedia stories, many of which are about everyday failures on the part of local officials such as lack of attention to irrigation sources (*Khabar Lahariya*, 2013), inability to access government housing benefits without paying bribes (*Khabar Lahariya*, 2019), governmental apathy regarding the spread of diseases such as tuberculosis (*Khabar Lahariya*, 2016), as well as deaths of over 1000 government school teachers who were put on polling duty for local elections during the COVID-19 pandemic (*Khabar Lahariya*, 2021). And it is such reporting, journalists from the outlet believe, that sets them apart from both local and urban mainstream outlets that occasionally "parachute" into the region to cover "big stories" on elections and droughts but rarely follow up (Splice Media, 2020).

In addition to such local accountability stories that make up a substantial portion of *Khabar Lahariya*'s coverage, the outlet has undertaken consistent coverage of complex issues such as the illegal mining and quarrying activities by the region's so-called sand mafia. Indeed, this in-depth "thematic" coverage—reflected in multiple stories from 2013 to the present— has resulted in accounts about the impact of such activities ranging from the experiences of locals who—in the absence of other employment opportunities—find themselves working in quarries, and the nexus between quarry owners and government officials (*Khabar Lahariya*, 2018) to investigations into the environmental degradation affecting farmers caused by illegal sand and stone mining (*Khabar Lahariya*, 2022).

Whereas local media fail to adequately cover the Bundelkhand region that has historically been characterized by political corruption and lack of development on the one hand and lawlessness and gang warfare on the other hand, *Khabar Lahariya* thus actively engages in a form of "investigative journalism from the grassroots" (Harcup, 2006, p. 133). As one of the founders of the paper put it:

> A lot of the reporting that we have been doing is uncovering scams between the local administration and politicians and these unlawful Robin Hoods and gang leaders. So, whereas local media has a vested interest in keeping those stories quiet because they get paid off by local administrations and also often protected by these gang lords, *Khabar Lahariya* is an independent platform which both ideologically and financially, is disrupting what the mainstream model is…
>
> (Splice Media, 2020)

Khabar Lahariya: Challenges and Impact

Not surprisingly, such disruption is not easily accepted and several of *Khabar Lahariya*'s reporters, many of whom operate as one-woman reporting bands, reprising the notion of Mojo reporters of the early digital era, have faced frequent harassment, threats and intimidation, typically from vested interests opposed to their work (Splice Media, 2020). Commenting on this, managing editor Meera Devi said:

> I have got threats against my life. There have been threats about shutting down our newspaper. They raise doubts about my reporting and investigate if I'm really a journalist. They intimidate and threaten because they are powerful. A lot of my colleagues have had mobs turn up at their homes and intimidate their families. They've caused our vehicles to be involved in crashes [by tampering or other means]. Now, that we are totally dependent on technology, [because we publish online] this intimidation is out in the open for everyone to see, in the form of trolling. If we post a story critical of someone, the trolls start piling up. Technology has provided them with a platform. I am always fearful for my life and for my family.
>
> (Pathak, 2021)

Nevertheless, the women reporters of *Khabar Lahariya* have continued to report. As one put it:

> How do I find the courage? Having entered this domain with a media organization which is counter intuitive to everything that we know in India, it comes with having made that decision…it's constant battle that you have with yourself, but if we lose courage, voices of women or other marginalized people will be silenced…
>
> (Splice Media, 2020)

In addition to such threats, financing has remained a consistent issue for the outlet—which has relied heavily on grants and philanthropic funding—from its inception. More recently, however the organization has been exploring new kinds of paid content as well as individual and institutional subscription models (personal communication, *Khabar Lahariya* team member, 2023) in order to put *Khabar Lahariya*'s reporting on a firm foundation, all the while, striving to remain independent of the myriad political and economic interests that permeate India's rural mediascape. Nevertheless, despite ongoing external and internal challenges, arguably, *Khabar Lahariya* has not only transformed the lives of its journalists (Splice Media, 2020) enabling them to challenge exclusions of caste and gender and narrate their own reality but has also contributed to an expansion of "public space" that did not previously exist in rural India, especially for women from marginalized communities.

Note

1 KL Hatke literally means KL different or apart but metaphorically speaking means KL plus or extra.

References

Agarwal, A. (2017, October 19). How this all-female-run publisher is using tech to bring news to rural India. *Medium*. https://medium.com/s/news-is-breaking/khabar-lahariya-492ddf852697

Allern, S. (2002). Journalistic and commercial news values: News organizations as patrons of an institution and market actors. *Nordcom Review, 23*(1–2), 137–152.

Ananya, I. (2016, August 16). *Khabar Lahariya,* now at a website near you. *News Laundry*. https://www.newslaundry.com/2016/08/16/khabar-lahariya-now-at-a-website-near-you

Atton, C. (2010). Alternative journalism: Ideology and practice. In S. Allan (Ed.), *Routledge companion to news and journalism* (pp. 169–178). Routledge.

Byerly, C. M., & Ross, K. (2006) Women and production: Gender and the political economy of media industries. In C. M. Byerly & K. Ross (Eds.), *Women and media: A critical introduction*. Blackwell Publishing.

Chambal Media (n.d.). 20 years of *Khabar Lahariya.* https://chambalmedia.com/khabar-lahariya/

Crenshaw, K. W. (1989). Demarginalizing the intersection of race and sex: A Black feminist critique of antidiscrimination doctrine, feminist theory and antiracist Politics. University of Chicago Legal Forum: 139–167.

Das, J. V. (2020). Women's community need papers. In K. Ross, I. Bachmann, V. Cardo, S. Moorti and M. Scarcelli (Eds.), *The international encyclopedia of gender, media, and communication*. Wiley. https://doi.org/10.1002/9781119429128.iegmc133

de Bruin, M. (2014). Gender and newsroom cultures. In A. V. Montiel (Ed.), *Media and gender: A scholarly agenda for the global alliance on media and gender* (pp. 49–56). UNESCO.

Dimitrova, D. V., & Neznanski, M. (2006). Online journalism and the war in cyberspace: A comparison between U.S. and international newspapers. *Journal of Computer Mediated Communication, 12*(1), 248–263.

Dixit, P. (2016, July 20). India's only all-woman rural newspaper has a new challenge: cracking digital publishing. *Factor Daily*. https://archive.factordaily.com/khabar-lahariya-digital-publishing/

Doshi, V. (2016, August 10). India's all-female paper goes digital to make gender taboos old news. *The Guardian*. https://www.theguardian.com/global-development/2016/aug/10/india-all-female-newspaper-khabar-lahariya-gender-taboos-old-news

Franklin, B., & Murphy, D. (1991). *What news? The market, politics and the local press*. Routledge.

Gerlis, A. (2008). Who is a journalist? *Journalism Studies, 9*(1), 125–128.

GIJN Staff (2022, July 18). Picking up pens was a revolutionary act: Telling the Stories of marginalized, rural women in India. *Global Investigative Journalism Network*. https://gijn.org/picking-up-pens-was-a-revolutionary-act-khabar-lahariya-gijn/

Hackett, R. A., & Carroll, W. K. (2006). *Remaking media: The struggle to democratize public communication*. Routledge.

Hall, S. (1973). The determinations of news photographs. In S. Cohen, & J. Young (Eds.), *The manufacture of news: Deviance, social problems and the mass media* (pp. 226–243). Constable.

Harcup, T. (2006). The alternative local press. In B. Franklin (Ed.), *Local journalism and local media: Making the local news* (pp. 129–139). Routledge.

Khabar Lahariya (2013, December 13). No water in irrigation canals. https://khabarlahariya.org/no-water-in-the-irrigation-canals/

Khabar Lahariya (2016, October 29). Banda village haunted by TB, Khabar Lahariya pulls curtain on administrative apathy. https://khabarlahariya.org/banda-village-haunted-by-tb-khabar-lahariya-pulls-curtain-on-administrative-apathy/

Khabar Lahariya (2018). If you are powerful, if you have connections with the authorities, you can do anything in Bundelkhand. https://www.youtube.com/watch?v=LfAwrn_ptTU

Khabar Lahariya (2019, August 3). Housing is only for people who can afford a bribe in UP's Sarumal. https://khabarlahariya.org/sarumal-lalitpur-village-pradhan-takes-bribe-for-p-m-awas-yojana/

Khabar Lahariya (2021, June 30). Losing you: Four families remember the teachers of Chitrakoot who died of Covid-19 from panchayat-poll duty. https://khabarlahariya.org/losing-you-four-families-remember-the-teachers-of-chitrakoot-who-died-of-covid-19-from-panchayat-poll-duty/

Khabar Lahariya (2022, November 11). Sand mining and sand mafia destroying crops of farmers. https://khabarlahariya.org/sand-mining-sand-mafia-destroying-crops-of-farmers-see-the-kavita-show-for-full-report/

Kitzinger, J. (1998). The gender politics of news production. In C. Carter, G. Branston, & S. Allan (Eds.), *News, gender and power* (pp. 186–203). Routledge.

Luepker, E. (2019, March 27). Newsmakers: Reporting in rural India with Kavita Devi. *Google News Initiative*. https://blog.google/outreach-initiatives/google-news-initiative/newsmakers-reporting-rural-india-kavita-devi/

Murti, A. (2020, October 31). Tell me more: Talking media ethics and representation with Kavita Devi, editor of *Khabar Lahariya*. *The Swaddle*. https://theswaddle.com/tell-me-more-talking-media-ethics-and-representation-with-kavita-devi-editor-of-khabar-lahariya/

Naqvi, F. (2007). *Waves in the hinterland. The journey of a newspaper*. Nirantar.

National Federation of Dalit Women (2009). Declaration. https://idsn.org/wp-content/uploads/user_folder/pdf/New_files/Key_Issues/Dalit_Women/NFDWdeclaration_2009.pdf

Newslaundry- (2022). Gender representation in Indian newsrooms. Gender representation in Indian newsrooms. https://www.themediarumble.com/reports

Ninan, S. (2007). *Headlines from the heartland: Reinventing the Hindi public sphere*. Sage Publications.

Pan, A. (2023). Gender, caste and subjectivity: Revisiting the #MeToo movement in India. *Feminist Encounters: A Journal of Critical Studies in Culture and Politics*, 7(1), 1–12. https://www.lectitopublishing.nl/download/gender-caste-and-subjectivity-revisiting-the-metoo-movement-in-india-12881.pdf

Park, J. (2020, November 19). *Khabar Lahariya*: India's rural watchdog with a feminist eye. *The Story*. https://medium.com/thestory-asiapacific/khabar-lahariya-indias-rural-watchdog-with-a-feminist-eye-6133df73abc6

Pathak, S. (2021, April 4). India's all-female news outlet faces sexism, death threats. *Capital Public Radio*. https://www.capradio.org/news/npr/story?storyid=980097004&__cf_chl_tk=53tDsZzNhWZ2M7L_Z7lgeanZJ0lzixoah478pcUWQZ8-1698702734-0-gaNycGzNDRA

Roy, M. (n.d.). Charting e-territory: How *Khabar Lahariya* made the digital transition. *Sarai*. https://sarai.net/charting-e-territory-how-khabar-lahariya-made-the-digital-transition/

Schirn Mag (2022, September 12). News from the fringes of Indian society. https://www.schirn.de/en/magazine/context/2022/gauri_gill/news_from_the_fringes_of_indian_society/

Sinha, A., & Malik, K. K. (2022). Women journalists of Khabar Lahariya and Namaskar: Enabling gendered media ecology in rural India. In A. Kaushik, & A. Suchiang (Eds.), *Narratives and new voices from India. Cases for community development and social change* (pp. 59–71). Springer.

Spivak, G. C. (1988). Can the subaltern speak? In C. Nelson, & L. Grossberg (Eds.), *Marxism and the interpretation of culture.* (pp. 66–111) University of Illinois Press.

Splice Media (2020). Diversity in media with *Khabar Lahariya.* https://www.splicemedia.com/stories/khabar-lahariya-building-newsroom-dedicated-to-diversity

Tomar, R. (2014). *Khabar Lahariya*: A feminist critique of mainstream Hindi print media. *Subversions, 2*(2). http://subversions.tiss.edu/vol2-issue2/ranu/

6 Concluding Note

A Brief Reflection on India's Alternative Journalisms Online

The notion that journalism should reflect the perspectives and interests of varied societal groups, especially those located on the peripheries of society, has considerable normative purchase, widely accepted by members of the profession as well as scholars and media observers alike. Indeed, even though the meanings of these terms remain contested, "the acknowledgement of pluralism and diversity, in different guises, can also be easily found in a variety of media policy declarations as well as ethical and professional guidelines of journalism" (Karppinen, 2018, p. 493). In the Indian context for instance, successive press commissions—regulatory bodies comprised of news industry representatives that were established in the post-independence period—have raised concerns regarding the need to ensure the presence of varied voices within the country's news media industry (Parthasarathi, 2021). However, despite such public affirmations as well as the "communicative abundance" (Keane, 2013)—manifest in the presence of an expansive media sector characterized by an exponential growth of news outlets since the 1990s—the media situation in India, particularly in terms of the existence of multiple perspectives, notably those that reflect the voices of economically and socially disadvantaged groups, continues to be troubling.

Indeed, Rao and Wasserman (2015) point out that the rise of commercial media—often celebrated as an indicator of media pluralism—has brought "its own set of constraints," whereby "some media organizations totally surrender to market forces by sensationalizing news and falling to the lowest common denominator of reporting" (pp. 651–652). Additionally, marginalized communities continue to be excluded from the mainstream media sphere along multiple axes ranging from "the structure and ownership of media, the demographic diversity of the journalistic workforce, to the selection and framing of individual news stories" (Karppinen, 2018, p. 497). As Anand (2005) argues, "print and visual media in India, like other privately controlled industries, do not believe in the principle of diversity." Expressed differently, the expansion of the Indian news industry as reflected in a growing number of media outlets has not resulted in more diverse newsrooms nor in more "radical journalism" that "aims to raise popular consciousness of wrongdoing, inequality, and the potential for change" (Christians et al., 2009, p. 126).

DOI: 10.4324/9781003244202-6

Instead, groups that face exclusion and discrimination on the grounds of caste, class, gender or faith in India are routinely subject to what philosopher Miranda Fricker (2007) terms epistemic injustice. As a concept, epistemic injustice refers to a specific form of injustice against "someone specifically in their capacity as a knower" (Fricker, 2007, p. 1) and offers insight into pervasive and often, systematic discrimination experienced by marginalized groups which by virtue of not being deemed epistemic agents, are denied opportunities to create knowledge and derive meaning from their social experiences. Although mainstream news organizations are by no means the only institutional drivers of epistemic injustice, their reporting which tends to underplay structural inequalities between groups, arguably contributes to disadvantaged groups and communities being "silenced within the democratic process or at least significantly constrained in voicing or pursuing their claims through it" (Harvey & Livingstone, 2000, p. 445). The end result, as Azam and Bhatia (2012) write, is that "for the rich and influential people, (Indian) democracy implies a right to justice, liberty and equality but for the poor, landless, tribals (Adivasis) and other marginalized groups, democracy is nearly empty" (p. 2).

But while professional journalism has done little to challenge the status quo of communicative power in the contemporary Indian context, this role has increasingly been taken on by the various forms of digitally produced alternative journalism explored in the preceding chapters. Distinguishable from professional news organizations in terms of content, adherence to canonical journalistic values and processes of news production, these emergent forms of news production seek both to explore and question the epistemic injustice experienced by groups such as Dalits, Muslims or women. More specifically, these alternative journalisms highlight the manner in which "unjust structures in meaning-making and knowledge producing practices" such as "exclusion and silencing; invisibility and inaudibility" as well as mis-representation (Kidd et al., 2017) embedded within the routines, practices and perspectives of mainstream professional journalism engender the silencing and exclusion of marginalized groups. Simultaneously, they also offer opportunities for active self-representation and participation by such subaltern groups within Indian society.

Challenging both the manner in which "media define for the majority of the population whatsignificant events are taking place," and their "powerful interpretations of how to understand these events" (Hall et al., 1978, p. 57), these digital alternative journalism outlets collectively seek to expand the "boundaries of consensus and promote exposure to critical voices and views that otherwise might be silenced in public debates" (Karppinen, 2018, p. 497). This is evident not only in their editorial choices and decisions but rather in their adoption of a different approach to journalism itself. Unlike mainstream outlets that are structurally oriented toward reflecting and prioritizing existing power hierarchies and preserving "the status quo of existing social consensus" (Karppinen, 2018, p. 504), these outlets instead seem to perceive journalism as a site of contestation and struggle. That is to say, they envisage the role of journalism as questioning "the existing socio-political order" and introducing "new perspectives that challenge the prevailing structures of power (Raeij-maekers & Maeseele, 2015, p. 1047). At a practical level, they seek to accomplish this goal through a reconceptualization of newsworthiness that centers the experiences of "the interests, views and needs of under-represented groups in society" (Atton, 2010, p. 169), an emphasis on "a different cast of voices in their stories" (Harcup, 2003, p. 360), so that ordinary people rather than a narrow range of elite or official sources serve as the so-called primary definers of reality, as well as by calling into question traditionally powerful "discursive nodes" such as objectivity and neutrality (Carpentier, 2005).

Of course, the state of digital alternative journalism is not entirely positive, with outlets facing a variety of ongoing challenges. For one, although growing cell phone penetration and the availability of low-cost broadband services has facilitated the rise of alternative journalisms online, uneven internet access as well as low levels of literacy especially in more remote rural regions of the country—where some of the most underprivileged communities are located—has implications for the growth of alternative journalism outlets. Moreover, the functioning and long-term sustainability of such outlets is also impacted by a lack of adequate financial resources. While this problem is not exclusive to alternative news outlets, it is exacerbated in their case by the fact that their primary audiences tend to be comprised of economically and socially marginalized communities who neither have the economic ability to provide subscription revenues nor do they constitute desirable target audiences for advertisers. And while in the past such outlets often received funds from international organizations and foundations, recent changes in governmental regulations have also inhibited the ability of such outlets to access such funds. The absence of stable revenue sources has obvious consequences for news outlets, particularly in terms of their ability to hire adequate staff and cover stories, both of which require significant investment of resources. Indeed, this point was made repeatedly by many of the journalists working for various digital alternative news sources, although a few newsworkers did acknowledge that developments such as low-cost AI solutions could be leveraged to enhance the news gathering and dissemination capabilities of their small newsrooms.

While the impact of these new technologies remains an unsettled question, it is important to recognize that despite limitations, India's digital alternative journalism outlets not only play a role in countering what Hall (1977) deemed the "ideological effect" of traditional news organizations but also offer challenges to "mass media's 'dominant discourses about reality … the interests of the dominant groups in society'" (Hebdige, 1979, p. 15). That is to say, they seem to operate from the position that although mainstream journalism serves as both driver and exemplar of dominant ideologies in society, this conjuncture is potentially open to change. Indeed, as Mouffe has noted, "the media are playing an important role in the maintenance and production of hegemony, but it is something that can be challenged" (as cited in Carpentier & Cammaerts, 2007, p. 5). The varied forms of digital alternative journalism emergent in India seek to undertake this task through actions that contribute to the creation of rips and fissures (Macgilchrist & Böhmig, 2012) within the country's hegemonic mainstream media formation, destabilizing it in ways that render it more open to the inclusion of varied voices and perspectives so critical to democracy.

References

Anand, S. (2005). A question of representation. Nieman Reports (Spring). https://nie-manreports.org/articles/a-question-of-representation/

Atton, C. (2010). Alternative journalism: Ideology and practice. In S. Allan (Ed.), *Routledge companion to news and journalism* (pp. 169–178). Routledge.

Azam, J., & Bhatia, K. (2012). Provoking insurgency in a federal state: Theory and application to India. Toulouse School of Economics Working Paper Series, 12-329, pp.1–45.

Carpentier, N. (2005). Identity, contingency and rigidity: The (counter-)hegemonic constructions of the identity of the media professional. *Journalism*, *6*(2), 199–219.

Carpentier, N., & Cammaerts, B. (2007). Hegemony, democracy, agonism and journalism: An interview with Chantal Mouffe. *Journalism Studies*, *7*(6), 964–975.

Christians, C.G., Glasser, T. L., McQuail, D., Nordenstreng, K., & White, A. W. (2009). *Normative theories of the media*. Illinois University Press.

Fricker, M. (2007). *Epistemic injustice: Power and the ethics of knowing*. Oxford University Press.

Hall, S. (1977). Culture, the media and the ideological effect. In J. Curran, M. Gurevitch, & J. Woollacott (Eds.), *Mass communication and society* (pp. 315–348). Arnold.

Hall, S., Critcher, C., & Jefferson, T. (1978). *Policing the crisis: Mugging, the state and law and order*. Palgrave Macmillan.

Harcup, T. (2003). The unspoken – Said: The journalism of alternative media. *Journalism: Theory, Practice, Criticism*, *4*(3), 356–376.

Harvey, C., & Livingstone, S. (2000). Protecting the marginalized: The role of the European Convention on Human Rights. *Northern Ireland Legal Quarterly*, *51*(3), 445–465.

Hebdige, D. (1979). *Subculture: The meaning of style*. Methuen.

Karppinen, K. E. (2018). Journalism, pluralism, and diversity. In T. P. Vos (Ed.), *Journalism. Handbooks of communication science*, no. 19 (pp. 493–510). de Gruyter.

Keane, J. (2013). *Democracy and media decadence*. Cambridge University Press.

Kidd, I. J., Medina, J., & Pohlhaus, G. (2017). Introduction. In I. J. Kidd, J. Medina, & G. Pohlhaus (Eds.), *Introduction to the Routledge handbook of epistemic justice* (pp. 1–14). Routledge.

Macgilchrist, F., & Böhmig, I. (2012). Blogs, genes and immigration: Online media and minimal politics. *Media, Culture & Society*, *34*(1), 83–100.

Parthasarathi, V. (2021). Dismembering media diversity: A tryst with two press commissions. *Media, Culture & Society*, *44*(3), 764–775.

Raeijmaekers, D., & Maeseele, P. (2015). Media, pluralism and democracy: What's in a name. *Media, Culture & Society*, *37*(7), 1042–1059.

Rao, S., & Wasserman, H. (2015). A media not for all. A comparative analysis of journalism, democracy and exclusion in Indian and South African media. *Journalism Studies*, *16*(5), 651–662.

Index

For Product Safety Concerns and Information please contact our EU representative GPSR@taylorandfrancis.com
Taylor & Francis Verlag GmbH, Kaufingerstraße 24, 80331 München, Germany